The Right to Write

The Literary Politics of Anne Bradstreet and Phillis Wheatley

Kathrynn Seidler Engberg

UNIVERSITY PRESS OF AMERICA,® INC.
Lanham • Boulder • New York • Toronto • Plymouth, UK

Copyright © 2010 by
University Press of America,® Inc.
4501 Forbes Boulevard
Suite 200
Lanham, Maryland 20706
UPA Acquisitions Department (301) 459-3366

Estover Road
Plymouth PL6 7PY
United Kingdom

Library of Congress Control Number: 2009925436
ISBN: 978-0-7618-4609-3 (paperback : alk. paper)
eISBN: 978-0-7618-4610-9

Dedicated with love
to my parents, William and Linda Seidler,
to my husband, Robert Engberg, and
to my son, Ethan Engberg

"Are there any lives of women?"

"No, my dear," said Mr. Sewell; "in old times, women did not get their lives written, though I don't doubt many of them were much better worth writing than the men's."

Harriet Beecher Stowe, *The Pearl of Orr's Island*

Contents

Preface

The Right to Write examines how a few women managed to enter into and succeed within the field of literary production, as well as gain authority and cultural capital in early America, despite restrictive social mores. Focusing specifically on the early American poets Anne Bradstreet and Phillis Wheatley, tracing their careers in seventeenth- and eighteenth-century America, I argue that they gained agency within a traditionally patriarchal field of literary production by utilizing their positions within society to network their selves into publication. Each woman wrote a plethora of verse, and their writing constitutes a major contribution to the development of the American literary canon. Using highly conventionalized heroic couplets, complicated rhyme and rhythm schemes, and classical allusions to disguise their political and personal agendas, Bradstreet and Wheatley emerged as powerful literary figures from very different positions within early American society. Each woman represents a unique way in which a majority of women writers negotiated their roles as both women and writers while influencing the political and social fabric of the new republic. Examining the context in which these women worked provides a window into the social conditions and aesthetic decisions they negotiated in order to write. Situating early American women writers within this context sheds light on how much influence they had on their own success and the ways in which they manipulated the market in their attempt to gain agency, writing their selves into the history of the newly emerging nation. This is not simply a historical and literary examination of the field of literary production; this study also provides new conceptions of early American women's writing that are valuable to feminist inquiry. This project is thus innovative in the way in which it recaptures a part of early American literary history.

Acknowledgments

The completion of this project is the conclusion of a journey. I owe a special debt to all of you who traveled with me on this journey. I owe a big thanks to my publisher, especially Samantha Kirk, who first contacted me and saw the value in this project. Thanks to all the folks at Alabama A&M University, my colleagues and my students for their support. I want to thank Dr. Phil Beidler, who has been an important mentor. His seminars further solidified my interest in early American literature and his loyal support, insights, guidance, and direction were paramount to the completion of this project. As a teacher, scholar, and most of all, a proud father, Dr. Beidler is an enormous influence on my life.

I want to thank Dr. Elizabeth Meese, Dr. Heather White, Dr. Edward Tang, and Dr. Pat Hermann for taking time to read, comment, and provide insight. I am grateful to Pat for also being my coach and friend. At the beginning of this process he taught me to run. Little did I know at the time how important the metaphor of "putting one foot in front of the other, even when it hurts," would be on this journey.

I also want to thank Dr. Henry Limouze for igniting my interest in 17th century literature and Dr. MaryBeth Pringle for first exposing me to early American women writers.

At my lowest points, what helped me move forward were the support of my family and friends. This journey has been made easier by my friends and I thank them for helping through some tough times. Thanks for the laughter, for grilling parties, for late night games of pool, for sharing life over coffee, for listening, and for keeping me on track. A big thanks to Nick (Superman), Mary, Nicholas, and Anna for providing a blue chair when I needed one, a cooked meal when there was nothing in my fridge, and a sense of family when my own was miles away. I am also grateful to Nick, another runner who "puts one foot in front of the other, even when it hurts," for helping me find my way back to God.

I am most indebted to my family. Both of my parents have stood strong when I was weak, read countless pages of material, spent numerous hours listening to ideas, worried, encouraged, and mostly just loved me as I worked on finishing this project and putting the pieces of my life back together. Thank you for encouraging me to be a strong, intelligent woman who can achieve her dreams—a priceless gift to give a child. I am also grateful to Rachel, Rob, Mary, Sarah, Steve, Mary Beth, and Dot Dot for their love and support.

The final steps of this journey would not have been possible without the help of my husband, Bob. I am appreciative of the hours he spent formatting the final manuscript. Mostly, I am grateful for his friendship and love. Thank you for loving so unconditionally and being my best friend.

And of course, there is my little "e". Ethan has been so good, while Mommy has been finishing up this manuscript. In the midst of writing, typing, and editing, you were so patient. Thank you for being such a wonderful kid and showing me the magic of being a mom. Thank you for a new journey.

A.M.D.G.

Introduction
Remember the Ladies

Woman must put herself into the text—as into the world and into history—by her own movement.

—Helene Cixous

On March 31, 1776, Abigail Adams wrote to her husband, John Adams, while he served as a delegate at the Continental Congress, admonishing him that "in the new Code of Laws . . . I desire you would Remember the Ladies and be more generous and favourable to them than your ancestors." John Adams responded, "As to your extraordinary code of laws, I cannot but laugh." Disgruntled by her husband's dismissal she wrote to Mercy Otis Warren,

> He is very sausy to me in return for a List of Female Grievances which I transmitted to him. I think I will get you to join me in a petition to Congress. I thought it was very probable our wise Statesmen would erect a New Government and form a new code of Laws. I ventured to speak a word in Behalf of our Sex, who are rather hardly dealt with by the Laws of England which gives such unlimited power to the Husband to use his wife ill.
>
> I requested that our Legislators would consider our case and as all Men of Delicacy and Sentiment are averse to Exercising the power they possess, yet as there is a natural propensity in Humane Nature to domination, I thought the most generous plan was to put it out of the power of Arbitrary and tyranick to injure us with impunity by Establishing some Laws in our favour upon just and Liberal principals.
>
> I believe I even threatened fomenting a Rebellion in case we were not Considered, and assured him we would not hold ourselves bound by any Law which we had neither voice, nor representation.
>
> (Harris 240)

Women worked to be included in the text called America from its earliest conceptualization. Although it took nearly two hundred years for women to finally be politically codified into the text of "We the People," some managed to have a literary voice and claim agency within a society that narrowly defined the role of women. How did such early literary women—poets especially—put themselves into the text of America, claiming the right to write and influencing the nature of the new nation?

With the first established press by Stephen Dayes in Cambridge, Massachusetts, in 1638, colonial women writers, alongside their male counterparts, made early efforts to write the first words of what would become a new republic. Over time many texts by these early female writers, even when available to contemporaries, became unavailable to readers with the rise of the modernist academic canon in the early part of the twentieth century. However, the onset of feminist inquiry over the past few decades has lead to a rediscovery and re-emergence of texts by early American women writers. The rediscovery of lost and neglected texts by literary scholars such as Nina Baym, Cathy Davidson, and Jane Tompkins has led to new editions and new insights into a large body of early American literary and cultural history that would otherwise have remained unrecognized. These texts by early American women are significant because they document the formation of the republic through diaries, novels, drama, poetry, and other genres, offering a critique of the projects of early American politics and literature from a woman's perspective. These texts are also significant because they offer a better understanding of the history of writing, reading, and authorship in early America. By recovering such forgotten literary history, we can better answer questions about our own technological shifts and how our modes of production affect writing and reading in contemporary America.

As these texts reemerge into print and critical study, the following question arises: How did these women negotiate their often tightly defined domestic roles with their pursuit of literary careers, within a very patriarchal climate, where women were not encouraged to write at all, let alone write and publish for a living? This study seeks to answer this question by examining the material conditions of being an author and reader during the seventeenth and eighteenth centuries in early America. In doing so, this study moves away from traditional formalist readings of texts and considers the book as an artifact, an object of material production situated within its historical context. More specifically, I will look at how the "game" of authorship was played, especially by these early American women, during a period when print was becoming the dominant, conventional mode of transmitting information. By studying the text as object as well as symbol, it is possible, as Wendy Wall notes, to "refine and problematize the representation of gender 'within' a work by noticing that gender is an issue at the level of commodity" (5). Using the case of *Gorboduc*, Wall explains that:

the preface's eroticization of the text provides a layer that complicates the way gender functions in the play. The text's "packaging," so frequently erased when a work's history is drained from it, speaks to the specific conditions by which meaning was and is transmitted. I pause in this study, then, to consider how a literary work becomes readable to its culture — to make visible the lens through which the "book" and the act of public writing are viewed. (5)

Extending her methodological concern to the relationship between the material and the symbolic, Wall argues "that the rhetoric itself can constitute crucial 'evidence' for making historical claims about literature and culture" (5).

Our own changes in print technology have led to new inquiries about the history of the "book," "authorship," and "reading." A new group of literary critics in France have explored "l'histoire du livre a l'histoire de la lecture" (Chartier 62). Francois Furet, one of the founders of the French schools of historiography, states in *The Workshop of History* that the study of the printed book "crystallizes all the difficulties of the historian's craft: the passage from the individual to the collective, the relation between the intellectual and the social, time's judgment on time, the measure of innovation and inertia" (99). The book becomes an object of historical analysis, inherently tied to the historical definitions of "author" and "reader." By studying texts as historical objects, we can get a better idea of how the "games of books and authors" were played, as Eisenstein argues in *The Printing Press as an Agent of Change* (121). More important, we can reconstruct the "historical context of generations whose conditions and expectations of authorship are so different from the present" and in turn "see the ways in which new questions arise and new models for literary history could be developed" (Ezell 3). By understanding past definitions of authorship and reading, we can better answer questions about our own conceptions of the process of reading and writing. Perhaps just as important as answering questions about our own technological shifts are the possibilities for uncovering lost works. As Margaret Ezell postulates:

> Such a mixed approach may seem to some too close to history or historical sociology to be considered literary in the classic sense; nevertheless, I feel confident that such multidisciplinary approaches may result not only in the recovery of "perished" authors, but also in a clarification in our sense of literary past as being "the past" and how it is distinct from the present.
>
> These approaches may also provide an opportunity to rethink our current assumption about who writes and who reads. (3)

Such an approach to literary scholarship may help to better answer questions about how we are going to preserve, archive, and canonize in an age of rapidly changing print technology.

Histories of print are often closely linked to histories of civil strife. Francis Bacon even advised that print, along with the compass and gunpowder, be studied, "For these three have changed the appearance of the world." The term "revolution" has been "formulaically joined to discussions of print technology" as the new (young, democratic) technology overthrew the established (old, aristocratic) one to usher in a new and better world (Ezell 7). Representative of this type of metaphorical construction of print is seen in Christopher Small's *The Printed Word: An Instrument of Popularity*, in which he directly links the nature of the new technology of printing presses and the English Civil War. He states that:

> Print as a means of spreading ideas among ordinary people assumed at this time a role so important, so indispensable, and so consciously used, that it became inextricably connected with the ideas themselves, and we find the right to print beginning to be claimed as a fundamental liberty, no less than those others which men were putting forward by its aid. Freedom of speech and freedom of print were formulated if not quite for the first time, with an unprecedented breadth of application, and the two went together, so much so that the differences between them (legal and other) were commonly ignored, and men demanded them as though the first naturally included the second. (23)

Small concludes that in England, in particular, "printing and political freedom were very closely linked; the unrestricted use of print was firmly associated with 'democracy'" (35).

The history of the material culture of authorship, the material experience of reading and writing, and studies into the nature of the literary marketplace and the history of the "book" itself have mostly been concerned with British literary texts. Studies include Wendy Wall's examination of authorship and publication in the English Renaissance, Margaret Ezell's study of the changing role of authorship in seventeenth-century England, and Clifford Siskin's investigation into literature and social change in Britain between 1700 and 1830. Other important studies include Nigel Smith's work on the pamphlet press during the English Civil War and Margaret Spufford's exploration of the scope of seventeenth-century chapbooks, which looks closely at penny presses, pamphlets, and popular literature, tracing the changes that occurred in readers' expectations of literacy standards. Sharon Achinstein looks at the ties between the English Civil War and the association with the printed word. Focusing specifically on Chaucer, Sidney, Spenser, Donne, and Milton, Kevin Pask looks at the contemporary "lives of poets" to trace "the emergence of the poet's life through its imbrication with early genres of life-writing" and the creation of a "professional" author in such texts (5).

With the exception of a few fragments of information scattered randomly in various critical texts, studies by scholars such as Philip Rounds, Emory Elliot, Robert Ferguson, and Michael Gilmore, there is no definitive study of the history of publication in early America, particularly with regard to the literary field of production for women. The significance of this project therefore lies in documenting that history to gain a better sense of how and why some colonial women writers "made it," along with discovering what publishing conditions were at the time. Examining the literary field of production in colonial America during the seventeenth and eighteenth centuries, this study will examine how a few women managed to enter into and succeed within the field of literary production, as well as gain authority and cultural capital. These are important issues if adequate comparisons are to be made between the modern field of literary production and past modes of production and if conclusions are to be drawn about whether or not the genders negotiate their contemporary roles differently from those of the past. This is not simply a historical and literary examination of the field of literary production; this study will also provide new conceptions of early American women's writing that will be valuable to feminist inquiry. This project is thus innovative in the way in which it recaptures a part of early American literary history.

Examining the context in which these women worked provides a window into the social conditions and aesthetics decisions they negotiated in order to "make it." Situating early American women writers within this context sheds light on how much influence they had on their own success and the ways in which they manipulated the market in their attempt to gain agency, writing their selves into the history of the newly emerging nation. Discouraged to pursue careers as writers, colonial women were relegated to fulfilling their duties as wives, mothers, and Christian matriarchs of their communities. If a woman tried writing as a profession, even in conjunction with her duties designated to her because of her gender, she was ostracized for not prizing her anonymity and her position as mother and wife within the community. Early American women such as Anne Yale Hopkins, for instance, who dared to take the considerable risk of stepping outside carefully defined roles in order to write were overtly ridiculed and dismissed, suffering malicious personal criticism. Yet some women managed to find agency and become professional writers despite restrictive social mores.

Focusing specifically on the early American poets Anne Bradstreet and Phillis Wheatley, tracing their careers in seventeenth- and eighteenth-century America, I argue that they gained agency within a traditionally patriarchal field of literary production by utilizing their positions within society to network their selves into publication. Each woman wrote a plethora of verse, and their writing constitutes a major contribution to the development of the American literary canon. Using highly conventionalized heroic couplets, complicated rhyme and rhythm schemes, and classical allusions to disguise their political and personal agendas, Bradstreet and Wheatley emerged as powerful literary figures from very different positions within early American society. Each woman represents a unique way in which a majority of women writers who "made it" negotiated their roles as both women and writers while influencing the political and social fabric of the new republic.

Anne Bradstreet, a member of the social and literary Puritan elite, is considered the first American female poet. Born in England, she married Simon Bradstreet and sailed to Massachusetts where they helped in the development of the new Bay Colony. Her husband became governor of the new colony, and she tended to the daily care of the family. In addition to her role as wife and mother, she wrote countless poems on religion, life in the New World, and family. Supposedly unknown to her, her brother-in-law, John Woodbridge, pastor of Andover church, brought with him to London a manuscript collection of her poetry and had it printed there in 1650. *The Tenth Muse* was the first published volume of poems written by a resident in the New World and was widely read. Chapter 1 examines how Bradstreet manipulated conventional poetic aesthetics and how she used her domestic connections to network herself into publication, while voicing her views on life in the New World.

Phillis Wheatley, a late colonial slave, is hailed as the first African American female poet. Brought to Boston in 1761 as a child, she was purchased by a wealthy tailor named John Wheatley to be a companion for his wife, Susannah. The Wheatley family associated with an enlightened group of Boston Christians who believed that slavery was incompatible with Christian life. Encouraged to write by the Wheatley family and prominent members of society, Phillis Wheatley published *Poems on Various Subjects, Religious, and Moral*, in 1773. Upon the publication of her poetry, eighteen prominent citizens testified that "under the Disadvantage of serving as a Slave in a Family in this Town," Wheatley "had been examined and thought qualified to write them." Chapter 2 examines how Phillis Wheatley used her position in society as a slave to advance her writing and politics. By exploiting her position as a slave and child prodigy, along with networking herself into the abolitionist movement, Wheatley became a spokeswoman for the cause of American independence and the abolition of slavery, thus providing for herself a platform from which to write.

Both Bradstreet and Wheatley managed to write themselves into mainstream culture, despite their gender, by ironically capitalizing on their gender, race, and social position. By using their domestic contacts in some form of self-effacement—often by taking advantage of their social status, usually obtained through marriage—these women published within the highly political, patriarchal field of literary production and claimed for themselves the right to write.

Examining the life and work of Anne Bradstreet and Phillis Wheatley is a good frame by which to study the shift from the manuscript coterie to the printed book. Bradstreet produced the first freestanding volume of poetry by a woman in 1650; Phillis Wheatley produced the second freestanding volume of poetry by a woman in 1773. Studying the evolution in technology in early America also means understanding how the field of production changed as the new nation emerged, especially for female writers trying to negotiate the marketplace.

One of the keys to understanding how the field of literary production changed lies in examining the definitions of authorship. Traditional literary histories, as Ezell criticizes, "have tended to behave as if the definition and classification of authorship that governs their own activities existed for earlier periods" (13). Ezell continues, "While it is acknowledged that the machines of production may be powered differently, it is also assumed, if not directly stated, that the human emotional or psychological dimension is a universal, transcendent phenomenon" (13). To take such a position would mean separating the act of authorship from the medium in which the writer worked. Just as separating a text from its historical setting erases the "conditions by which meaning was and is transmitted," separating the act of authorship from the medium in which the writer worked limits the possibilities for understanding the circumstances influencing the ways in which the writer negotiates the field of publication, which directly affects the "packaging" and aesthetics of the text.

During the seventeenth and eighteenth centuries, in both Old and New England, the category of "author" was an unstable one. As contemporary readers of these texts, we must understand authorship in its more elevated literary sense by seeing it as intricately linked to textual transmission and to the ways in which this was understood and represented. Authorship, even in early America, thus emerges in the collision between manuscript and print practices, and between aristocratic amateurism and the marketplace. The notions of "authority" and "agency" blur as well, since they are necessarily associated with authorship. Therefore, to study the climates in which Bradstreet and Wheatley wrote is also to examine the possible ways in which they controlled their social construction as the definitions of "reader," "writer," "author," and "agent" changed.

I chose 1650 to begin this study because it not only marks the year the first freestanding volume of poetry was published in early America, but the mid-seventeenth century is credited by scholars as the "birth of a modern cultural era." Prior to the late sixteenth century, manuscript transmission, patronage, and even the categories of "reader" and "writer" remained relatively static and fixed. The historian Colin Clair notes that the technology of print was available to writers in England for more than a hundred years, but it was not until the late 1500s that print became "Englished." Native printers began to cut their own type and produce their own paper, a new commodity dependent on the trade with British colonies throughout the world (Clair 1-2). British colonies produced the large crops that could sustain the emerging book market. Writers began "to find it advantageous to circulate their names and texts through a more far-reaching medium when print production became cheaper and the literacy rate increased at the turn of the century" (Wall 14). H. S. Bennett documents in *English Books and Readers 1558-1603* that the number of printed titles nearly doubled between 1558 and the 1580s, with an increase from 54 titles in 1500, to 125 in the mid-1500s, to 202 titles by 1580. Bennett notes that for every four items published in the first two decades of Elizabeth's reign, there were six published in the last two decades (269-71).

The rapid increase in production and its affordability not only solidified a new, broader readership but gave rise to new social tensions evident in the competing modes of production—manuscript versus print. Manuscript transmission had remained relatively unchanged for centuries and helped to delineate the cultural elite. The act of reading and writing was an act of social classification—until the invention of the press. Manuscript allowed for strict censure. Writing, especially poetry, was a courtly act. As Wall explains, "At a time in which the economic and cultural world was shifting to accommodate a 'middling' class, people at many points on the social spectrum were concerned with both social mobility and the security of status indicators. Regardless of the actual cultural effects of printing, textual transmission became rhetorically tied to the symbolic codes that designated rank" (12). Manuscript writing, particularly poetry, was "seen to constitute a bid for gentility" (12). Alvin Kernan, in his important study of Samuel Johnson and print, characterizes manuscript texts as "polite or courtly letters—primarily oral, aristocratic, amateur, authoritarian, court-centered," whereas the newly emerging print was a "market-centered, democratic literary system" (4).

The "gentility" feared the rising use of print since it seemed to threaten their elite position. Renaissance texts "air complaints that professional writers might ascend to the aristocracy and become the cultural trendsetters of their day or alternately, that printing would render courtly practices obsolete because anyone with money could partake of social jokes, debates, and conversations" (Wall 12). The shift from manuscript coterie to print blurred the boundaries that separated the aristocracy from the lower gentry. In *English Society, 1580-1680*, Keith Wrightson examines the social, political, and economic shifts in British society. He states that publication was perceived with real fear and anxiety because it represented the threatening problem of social reorganization; print was associated with demographic, economic, legal, and administrative changes in early modern England (72). These changes ultimately led to the English Civil War and, it can be argued, resulted in the American Revolution as well.

The modes of textual transmission defined communities in early modern England. At the same time, transmission of texts, whether by manuscript coterie or print distribution, was a crucial decision for the writer. Choosing manuscript or print became a marketing decision—which in some cases could mean life or death, depending on the content of the text being distributed. With increasing censure by the monarchy, along with the aristocracy's desire to maintain their elite status, print became synonymous with vulgarity and sexual promiscuity, with the hope of deterring readers from participation. During the periods of unchallenged Stuart rule, under the reigns of James I and Charles I, censorship was at its most draconian. The Stationers Company, established by King James I, was responsible for preventing the publication of offensive writing (Love 187). According to its charter, the Stationers Company had complete jurisdiction over religious writing. Printed religious material, including books, was supposed to be submitted to ecclesiastical licensors (Greg 1-4). In 1643, the method of censorship was reviewed. Parliament replaced the old ecclesiastical licensing arrangement with a new one under which all works intended for the press had to be approved by licensors appointed by itself (Siebert 213). It is this 1643 licensing act that John Milton attacks in *Aeropagitica*.

During the reign of Charles II, censure of public texts was handled with veracity, as writers and booksellers distributing printed material illegally were thought to be committing treason, an act punishable by death. Under the Licensing Act of 1662, Charles II brought licensing under his complete control. Roger L'Estrange was appointed to the post as the full-time licensor levied by Charles II himself, with powers of investigation and seizure (Siebert 214). Though the act was allowed to lapse from May 1679 to June 1685, and finally dropped for good in 1695, official control over the presses was apparent. Once a book appeared in print, either legally or illegally, powerful means of suppression were available. According to Love, "Punishments of great ferocity were inflicted on authors, printers, and booksellers under the laws of treason, libel and *scandalum magnatum* (the libeling of peers), and seizures could be organized in sufficiently disciplined communities" (188). Only during the English Civil War and the Exclusion crisis did writers of all political persuasions come closer than at any other period in the seventeenth century to a contemporary conception of open public debate (Greg 1-4).

Though print was regulated with fervent censure, it did represent a more democratic form of distribution, since it was not relegated to the privacy of the coterie. Lois Potter, in *Secret Rites and Secret Writing: Royalist*

Literature, 1641-1660, describes how Cavalier writers of the interregnum developed a subtle set of interpretative codes, allowing the public text to be read in a factional way. Readers created communities of individuals willing to acknowledge and impose such codes (87). The clergy who were ejected from their livings under the Commonwealth or the 1662 Act of Uniformity demonstrate how the presses could distribute freely outside the boundaries of government censure. The 1662 act insisted that clergy take oaths of allegiance to William and Mary. Clergy who refused were removed from their stations in the pulpit. Denied the pulpit, they turned to printed tracts as a substitute for the spoken sermon, circulating copies gratis to those who could not afford to pay for them and using the presentation of specially bound copies to wealthy sympathizers as a form of fund-raising (Patterson 98). In cases such as this, printed text gave rise to "communities of the book." Love reinforces the power of the press to organize communities of people, noting that:

> [t]he advent of the subscription list late in the [seventeenth] century made these communities publicly visible while strengthening the political dimension of book purchase. In an age when the bookseller was also the publisher, the clientele of a particular shop might form a community in its own right, cemented by common tastes and regular meetings at the source of supply. (183)

Since print is an article of commerce, it can reach large numbers of readers and is more difficult to regulate. Print's power to mobilize clearly fueled increasing anxieties in the aristocracy and made clear the need to censure.

Suppression of print by the strict licensing acts did not necessarily thwart the production of dissident texts. Courageous, ideologically committed writers found other means to publish their work, often circulating oppositional texts scribally, since manuscript transmission provided a safer avenue than print. The transmission history of John Donne's *Biathanatos* clearly illustrates how scribal (manuscript) transmission offered him protection from public scrutiny. In this famous treatise, written in 1607-08, Donne argues that suicide is not in all circumstances to be condemned. Because this was a radical concept, Donne was very cautious about who was allowed to see the manuscript; he made sure that it was not published through the press. In a letter dated 1619 to Sir Robert Ker Donne writes, "[N]o hand hath passed upon it to copy it, nor many eyes to read it: only to some particular friends in both Universities, then when I writ it, I did communicate it" (xli). Similar to Alexander Pope's *Pastorals*, Donne's treatise was "published" by allowing a series of readers to view the manuscript. Donne's desire to control or censure the text from readers is clarified in a later statement in the same letter to Ker. Donne insists, "Reserve it for me, if I live, and if I die, I only forbid it the Presse, and the Fire" (xlvi-xlvii). Put simply, only upon the event of his death should the text be treated as published, and it should be published only through the scribal medium. Some years later, at the request of Lord Herbert of Cherbury, Donne allowed another copy to be made. Donne maintained careful social control over which community of readers would "lay eyes on the text."

To consider manuscript transmission as "publishing" begs the following question: Was Donne's publishing of his treatise a "public" or "private" transaction? It is this blurring of definitions that is so indicative of literary production in seventeenth-century England. What is certain is that manuscript transmission gave Donne the freedom to circumvent possible "public" censure, scrutiny, and perhaps even punishment by keeping his text within his own "private" scribal community.

Writers who still chose to publish their work and distribute using the public press disassociated themselves from their texts. Writers often claimed that their work was published "without their knowledge." If a writer chose print, then it was essential for him to follow the decorum that governed the public utterances, if he were to remain a "gentleman." To appear in print meant dressing suitably for readers. The stigma of print made writing difficult for both male and female writers, although the vulgarity associated with print culture was particularly cruel to women writers who wanted to keep their modesty intact, which was important if one were to succeed socially. Anne Finch, Countess of Winchilsea, praised Lady Pakington, the author of *The Whole Duty of Man*, as having combined the "Skill to write" with the "Modesty to Hide" (56-9). The alternative to "hiding" or "masking" oneself as a writer was to draw a metaphorical equation between printing one's text and sexual immorality, as seen in the following lines by Richard Lovelace:

> Now as her self a Poem she doth dresse,
> And curls a Line as she would do a tresse;
> Powders a Sonnet as she does her hair,
> Then prostitutes them both to publick Aire. (200)

To publish, especially as a woman writer, was to prostitute one's self, an act that could result in social ruin.

It is this illicit sexual metaphor associated with print distribution that kept many women from entering into the field of production through the print medium. Instead they relegated themselves to scribal transmission. Two good examples of women writers who chose to remain in the realm of manuscript coterie and who precede Anne Bradstreet as contemporaries by a couple of decades are Lady Mary Wroth and Mary Sidney, Countess of Pembroke. After encountering trouble over the print publication of her 1621 roman à clef, *The Countesse of Montgomery's Urania*, Lady Mary Wroth kept the second part of her poem and a play derived from it in manuscript (Wroth 28-38).

Mary Sidney maintained tight control over the work of her brother, Sir Philip Sidney. Sir John Harington complains in his *Treatise on Play* that keeping Sidney's poems confined to manuscript distribution was too restrictive. He writes:

> Seing it is allredy prophecied those precious leaues (those hims that she doth consecrate to Heauen) shall owtlast Wilton walls, meethinke it is pitty they are unpublished, but lye still inclosed within those walls lyke prisoners, though many haue made great suyt for theyr liberty. (Rathmell xxvii-xxix)

The Sidneian psalms were never printed. Keeping the poems in the scribal medium ensured that Mary Sidney would remain the constant improver of the work, a role that furthered her own writing career since it was she who received most requests for copies. This role of gatekeeper gave her access to social circles that would support her own work. This also allowed her to tightly control audience, specifically in terms of who would be able to receive a copy, a move that made the poems even more popular.

Katherine Philips, perhaps the most well-known female poet of the seventeenth century, built her reputation through manuscript transmission. Known as Orianda by her circle of readers, Philips distributed her poems among intimate friends in Ireland and later expanded to a wider readership throughout court. The scribal medium allowed Philips to closely guard her reputation in court and, like Mary Sidney, manuscript transmission furthered her writing career, since she wrote poems specifically addressed to many members of her own coterie. Elaine Hobby offers insight into Philips's calculated reasons for distributing her work in manuscript form only, explaining:

> In part, the image of Orianda that has come down to us is dependent on the belief that her writing was really a secret and private affair, her poems passed around only in manuscript form to a few trusted friends. This is an anachronistic distortion of the method of "publication" that she used: circulation of manuscripts was the normal way to make writing public before widespread use of printed books, and was a method that continued to be popular in court circles throughout the reign of Charles II, at least.
>
> Such a description also fails to consider the fact that, as a royalist poet married to a leading parliamentarian, she had positive reasons for avoiding too much public attention during the 1650s, which was when she did most of her writing. Bearing these factors in mind, we find that the evidence suggests that she was actually a well-known writer. . . . The "public" she was interested in reaching was the coterie of court and leading poets, not the wider world. (129)

Manuscript protected Philips from possible attacks on her reputation. She was so concerned about this that when an unauthorized edition was printed in 1664, she desperately tried to have it suppressed. Philips knew that distributing her work in print would not give her the freedom to censure her own readership, because she could not control who read her work if it was published on the press. Carefully controlling her persona and maintaining it in the scribal medium offered her greater opportunity to socially network and maintain the quality of her work. Ultimately manuscript transmission offered the greatest freedom for Katherine Philips, along with many of her contemporaries, providing them with a safe avenue to become writers. The scribal medium protected their reputations and offered them the critical social networking needed to distribute their work.

When situating Anne Bradstreet within this literary history of the seventeenth century and comparing her experience to the writing careers of many of her contemporary female British counterparts, it is clear that *The Tenth Muse* was an exception. Although Bradstreet claimed that her book was published without her knowledge, what becomes most evident is that it did not remain within the manuscript coterie. Manuscript transmission may have offered many of her contemporaries safety from public ridicule and censure, but in the case of Anne Bradstreet, print actually afforded her more freedom. By distributing her work in print she was able to circumvent the volatile religious politics within the Massachusetts Bay Colony, offering her a safe platform from which she could espouse her own views. Other women, including her sister, were condemned for holding private meetings and distributing manuscripts that discussed alternative religious views. Bradstreet's father, Governor Thomas Dudley, refused to tolerate such freedom of speech, especially from women, and did little to protect his own daughter Sarah. In this study, I examine the historical and political context in which Bradstreet was writing and the ways in which Bradstreet used the transition from manuscript to print technology in the seventeenth century to protect her reputation, while contributing to public discourse within the colonies, an action that placed her at great risk. By controlling the material production of the text, during this time of rapid transition from manuscript to print, Bradstreet transcended her prescribed role as a Puritan woman, becoming instead a public reformer who argued for political and religious toleration in seventeenth-century America.

The stage for writers, particularly women, changed significantly by the mid-eighteenth century during the Restoration. The stage for black writers, especially slave women, was nearly nonexistent. Mass printing distribution in the American colonies and in Britain finally transitioned into a preferred commercial trade. Manuscript transmission was transformed into fashionable parlor games. The outdated technology represented a fading aristocratic possession of the world of letters; the older practice of circulating scribal texts was instead a choice" (Ezell "Social" 12). Book-making had become a business. The lapse of the 1695 Licensing Act and the institution of the first copyright act in 1709 allowed printers and booksellers to retain control of perpetual copyrights by means of auctions open only to members of the trade who were licensed by Parliament (Feather 74). By 1774, copyright law broadened further, as advocates of commercialization rallied Parliament to pass an act permitting booksellers without "perpetual copyright" interests in stock print and the ability to publish at will, creating more of a "free market" system than the present monopoly in print trade (Feather 57-65). New print standards commodified the private coterie, reconstructing the culture of reading and writing.

Print technology enlarged the scope of reading and writing, and in turn, as Julie Stone Peters's study of Congreve describes, writing and literacy became "strongly identified with print, and the Restoration had a sense of a world overflowing with the productions of the press" (15). The proliferation of reading and writing created a demand for more writers. For the first time, commercial authorship became a profession. Writers such as Swift, Addison, Johnson, and especially Pope took the stage, claiming their roles as professional authors. The expansion of writers in turn created more readers, and audiences broadened to include the middle class and marginalized groups, including women.

It is important to note that while the market of commercial print was rapidly expanding, printed material rarely meant the publication of books. Books were still relatively scarce, especially in the American colonies. Most books were published in Britain, and most were books of verse (Emerson 14). Prior to the American Revolution, paper was of such poor quality that it was suitable only for broadsides, newspapers, and other matter whose anticipated life was short. Printers in England did not suffer from a lack of quality paper, although it was expensive. But British printers realized that the market of rapid exchange was a more profitable pursuit than book publishing.

Margaret Ezell writes in her study, *Social Authorship and the Advent of Print*:

> It is important . . . to see what type of author actually did get into print during this period. Of the 3,550-plus printed texts so far counted that appeared between 1666 and 1680, . . . more than half of them were single sermons or tracts (which should alert us from the start that genre and subject matter will be as significant a factor as "class" in determining who embraced the new technology and who held fast to the old) . . . it should be noted that, of these more than three thousand titles, pamphlets and small books made up the vast majority of the sum after sermons. (13)

Jerome Friedman concludes that broadside ballads "were the most popular printed format in England" (7). Presses made mass, dispersible, and rapid distribution possible, and therefore printers preferred more disposable forms of print production to meet the demand for quickly printed high volumes of copy. Readers became subscribers, as printers solicited money, securing funds to produce "installments" of text, leaving readers hungry to consume more and increasing demand.

Changes in literary production led to redefinitions of once fixed class modalities in England and in the American colonies. The proliferation of literacy, the act of reading, enabled those not empowered to consider themselves "equal" subjects with the elite precisely because they could read. Individuals who were previously politically powerless became users of print, expressing themselves by participating in the social exchange of economy and ideas, contributing to the fluidity of once prescribed hierarchically inscribed roles (Feather 18). Edward Countryman indicates that "radical politics and nascent class consciousness foundered on electoral participation and on the spirit of voluntary association" in New York during the 1780s (294). Reading became a diplomatic process, allowing anyone to participate in the electoral process. By engaging in acts of community building, and by reading about their actions, would-be elites could create a social imaginary in which they could perceive themselves as operating from an equal position with elites. As Carla Mulford describes, "To phrase it another way, the urgency of the needs of non-elite groups of people was to some extent expelled by their increasing literacy. Members of the less well-to-do circles could, in the act of reading, create for themselves a social imaginary in which they could circulate as 'equal' members" (25).

Publications produced as magazines, newspapers, and broadsides increased the participatory process. David Paul Nord argues in his study on magazine reading during the eighteenth century that:

> The magazine might be viewed as another arena for popular participation, in this case participation in the formerly elite culture of science and education, arts and letters, virtue and honor, cultucation and character. The values of the magazine were traditional; it was the participation of the working class that was new. (115)

Subscribers and purchasers of print were not just the Washingtons, Jeffersons, and Adamses of the United States or the countesses, dukes, and lords of upper-class Britain; they were barbers, butchers, merchants, and women. Christopher Small's study makes a direct link between the nature of the new print technology and the English Civil War, stating that:

> Print as a means for spreading ideas among ordinary people assumed at this time a role so important, so indispensable, and so consciously used, that it

became inextricably connected with the readers themselves, and we find the right to print beginning to be claimed as a fundamental liberty, no less than those others which men were putting forward by its aid. Freedom of speech and freedom of print were formulated if not quite for the first time, with an unprecedented breadth of application, and the two went together, so much so that the differences between them (legal or other) were commonly ignored, and man demanded them as though the first naturally included the second. (23)

Small concludes that "printing and political freedom were very closely linked; unrestricted use of print was firmly associated with 'democracy'" (35). Print technology allowed individuals to move, as Benjamin Franklin's death note attested, "from small and low beginnings, to . . . high rank and consideration among men," offering a new range of participation in the exchange of public discourse. The proliferation of print resulted in a more "democratic" form of literary participation, while also giving rise to a readership who clamored for increasingly colorful, entertaining, and unexpected genius. The Englishman William Shenstone wrote in 1761, "The public has seen all that art can do, and they want the more striking efforts of wild, original, enthusiastic genius."

In 1773, the appearance of *Poems on Various Subjects, Religious and Moral* by Phillis Wheatley, Negro Servant to Mr. John Wheatley, of Boston, in New England, provided English readers with the latest "unexpected genius." A review of Wheatley's new book in the September 1773 *London Magazine* commented:

These poems display no astonishing power of genius; but when we consider them as the production of the young untutored African, who wrote them after six months [*sic*] casual study of English language and of writing, we cannot suppress our admiration of talents so vigorous and lively. We are the more surprised too, as we find her verses interspersed with the poetical names of the ancients, which she has in every instance used with strict propriety. (Mason 24)

The significance of Wheatley's achievement is framed by her prescribed role as a slave; without her position she may not have been considered "astonishing."

By situating Phillis Wheatley within the historical context of eighteenth-century literary production and the political climate of early America in the mid-1700s, her "genius" as a writer becomes even more apparent to the contemporary reader. Although many assessments portray Wheatley as "selling out," I argue that reducing Wheatley to such terms misses the highly political nature of her work, and it misses the astonishing ways in which she advanced herself. In this study, I examine how on the surface her poetry may appear to be a passive gesture, but by "selling" herself she actually "buys" herself, both literally and figuratively. By appearing in print as a slave, read by audiences in both the colonies and Britain, Wheatley's poetry becomes a profoundly political and polemical gesture. Wheatley moved outside the boundaries of her prescribed role as a slave woman by "selling" herself, which in turn eventually led to her manumission. She made herself appealing to her readership by employing popular eighteenth-century poetic devices, while also carefully using her social connections to network herself among the elite on both sides of the Atlantic. Wheatley, I argue, used abolitionist politics, along with the political tensions of Old and New England during the American Revolutionary period, to advance her own personal agenda. Wheatley's seeming embrace of "whiteness" and "passivity" was a subtle publishing strategy to gain social agency, which ultimately provided the necessary leverage she needed to participate in cultural exchange and argue for political change—a bold move for a female slave. In the end, however, she became an eighteenth-century icon and, more important, she gained her freedom.

Bradstreet and Wheatley took great risk by challenging their roles as early American women. They wrote during a time of enormous technological and political change. They managed to put themselves "into the text" of America and "into history" by claiming their right to write. It is important to reconstruct the historical climate of writers such as Bradstreet and Wheatley if we are going to adequately confront our own rapidly changing modes of literary production and definitions of authorship in the twenty-first century.

Chapter One

Anne Bradstreet:
With Her "owne sweet hand"

Your only hand those Poesies did compose,
Your head the source, whence all those springs did flow,
Your voice, whence changes sweetest notes arose,
Your feet that kept the dance alone, I trow

—John Rogers, 1678

This story begins in 1650. A young woman awoke one morning to discover that she was an author as a result of the actions of her brother-in-law. Allegedly without her consent, he abducted her text and carried the bundle to England where it was printed by Stephen Bowtell in Popes Head-Alley, the center of liberal book trade in London. Suddenly, Anne Bradstreet became the first person to publish a freestanding book of poetry in the New World. *The Tenth Muse: Lately Sprung up in America* became an important piece of early American literary history. To be sure, its place in the history of American literature is solid. Bradstreet's book is the first volume of poetry published by a British American living on "American" soil. Having gone through five editions and two reprints, it appears in every American literature anthology. Her work has proven more durable than that of many of her English female contemporaries; their poetry, though more popular in their time, has been neglected or forgotten.

According to the conventional story, this book seems to have "sprung" from nowhere. In the preface to *The Tenth Muse*, John Woodbridge, the brother-in-law who "abducted" the text, insists:

It is the Work of a Woman, honoured, and esteemed where she lives, for her gracious demeanor, her eminent parts, her pious conversation, her courteous disposition, her exact diligence in her place, and discreet managing of her Family

1

occasions, and more so, these Poems are the fruit but of some few houres, cur-
tailed from her sleep and other refreshments. I dare add little lest I keep thee too
long; if thou wilt not believe the work of these things (in there kind) when a man
sayes it, yet believe it from a woman when thou seest it. This only I shall annex,
I fear the displeasure of no person in the publishing of these Poems, but the Author, without whose knowledg, and contrary to her expectation, I have presumed
to bring to publick view, what she resolved in such a manner should never see
the Sun. (Ellis 84)

Woodbridge's admission to secretly printing the text and his adamant defense
of Bradstreet's character as a dutiful Puritan wife and mother who never
neglects her domestic duties allowed Bradstreet to avoid possible condemnation from the community. He shifted authority over the text to himself, which
allowed Bradstreet to maintain a private, anonymous self that was indicative
of a good Puritan woman; she became the unknowing "authoress" who had
little control over what "sprung" up.

This is a great story, but Woodbridge's absconding with the text without
Bradstreet's consent appears suspiciously contrived when we look beyond
his surface apologies and examine various poems in *The Tenth Muse* closely.
The book is riddled with clues that tell a very different story—one of a
woman desiring to contribute to the transatlantic and local conversations in
the Bay Colony regarding religious and political reform who consciously and
deliberately wrote, compiled, and even denied her own text to ensure that she
maintained her legitimacy in society as a "good" Puritan woman. Aware that
her audience condemned other women of her community who stepped out of
their prescribed roles, such as her sister, Sarah Dudley, and Anne Hutchinson,
Bradstreet coyly, but expertly, used the changing nature of the field of literary
production in both New and Old England to "sell" both herself and her text
to her desired audience.

To understand the nature of Bradstreet's work and how she "made it" during a time when women, and even men, were scorned for voicing political
and religious ideas that challenged the majority, especially if they appeared in
print, her text must be situated within the proper publishing context. Instead
of performing close readings of individual poems or narrowing Bradstreet to
categories unrepresentative of her intentions, we must see her as a participating member of a transatlantic Anglo-American writing community that was
experiencing revolutionary religious and political reform during a period of
rapid transition from manuscript coterie culture to mass printing distribution.
When placed within this context, the polemical nature of *The Tenth Muse* becomes clear: Bradstreet's book was an argument for political change regarding censure and toleration of difference. By publicly espousing her views,
Bradstreet gained social agency by carefully and deliberately embracing her

social role, utilizing her social connections to gain agency in the male-dominated field of literary production.

I. TO BE A WOMAN IN PRINT: PREFATORY POLITICS

Piecing together the story of Anne Bradstreet's emergence as the first "American" poet begins with examining all the prefatory material, print and otherwise, that frames her first edition. The need to delineate editions for this study is necessary because the second edition, published posthumously, contains not only revisions Bradstreet started to make but also works her children felt should be included. In the second edition her children took the liberty of editing and adding to the original body of text, including what are often called her "domestic" poems, private meditations about her husband, her role as wife and mother, and her children. The 1650 edition was published while Bradstreet was still able to self-fashion the text and includes only her politically and religiously philosophical works.

Although Bradstreet was one of the first settlers of the Massachusetts Bay Colony and became the wife of the governor of the new colony, she also saw herself as a member of a relatively elite English society. She left her Lincolnshire home and emigrated to the New World as a young bride at the age of nineteen. Although divided from her birthplace by an ocean, Bradstreet was influenced greatly by her homeland upbringing, and she remained heavily involved in the ongoing disputes regarding the English Civil War and the restoration of Charles II, as well as the ongoing religious conflicts, as observed in poems such as "Old England, New England." Placing her within this historical context as a member of a transatlantic community enables us to better understand the nature of her work.

Raised in the privileged English home of the Earl of Lincolnshire, Bradstreet had direct access to and was influenced by the art and writing of the Renaissance. The family library contained well over eight hundred volumes, a considerable holding for the time. Bradstreet had family connections to elite society as well; she was indirectly related to Mary Sidney, Countess of Pembroke and sister of Sir Philip Sidney, who helped translate Sidney's psalms, adding her own prefatory poem, "To the Angell spirit of the most excellent Sir Phillip Sidney," which she presented to Queen Elizabeth in 1599.

Thus, Bradstreet was not just as a colonial figure in New England but a participating member of English society. This context provides the appropriate backdrop for reading her work and understanding the politics of how she became a participant in public discourse. As part of her education, Bradstreet read her "elite" contemporaries. Civil conversation was a vital component for

English men and women to accept the social fragmentation that had resulted from rapid population growth, inflation, polarization of wealth, increasing poverty, and general fear of disorder resulting from the brewing civil war.

One mode of participating in such discourse was through the coterie culture of hand-to-hand manuscript exchange, or newly published books, specifically poetry. Adhering to Renaissance ideals, the lyric was still considered the most formal and acceptable form of civil conversation. As a daughter of the Renaissance, Bradstreet in *The Tenth Muse* uses common poetic devices indicative of Renaissance poetic aesthetics. Examined through this historical lens, we can better examine how Bradstreet created the opportunity to publish, gaining the social agency needed to "sell" the text to readers in a public market.

Most lengthy Renaissance books of poetry begin with prefatory material; Bradstreet's text is no different. English Renaissance scholars such as Helen Wilcox, Margaret Ezell, and Wendy Wall all argue that Renaissance English poets, especially women, can be understood through the written self-portraits and prefatory material frequently used to legitimize both writer and text. They argue the preface is a significant opportunity for authorial self-construction, and this is particularly so in the early modern period in England when the relationship of a text to a chosen literary genre, and of the writer to a chosen patron is traditionally established (Wilcox 200). What Jonathan Swift referred to as the "porch," the prefatory material shifts the text and reader from the private coterie culture, where text is physically passed from hand to hand, receiving oral commentary, to the public world of literature, where text is printed and distributed as a commodity. This shift in print culture made the prefatory material extremely important since it gave writers a chance to shape readers' expectations before entering the work, providing writers with a vital opportunity to justify why they wrote, and establishing themselves as "authors." For the Renaissance writer, Wilcox argues that "all of this must be achieved through a rhetoric of modesty and self-denial; the authorial image in the Renaissance preface, male or female, is conventionally that of the reluctant and apologetic public speaker" who is "made" public unintentionally, without personal consent (15).

Like many of her female contemporaries writing in England, such as Amelia Lanyer, Mary Sidney, and Katherine Philips, Bradstreet crafted her prefatory gesture as a clash between self-deprecation and self-justification, revealing, as Susan Wiseman suggests, "a particular self-consciousness" among women writers regarding their texts being gendered, thus highlighting women writers' need to negotiate prevailing concepts of feminine decorum (Wiseman 12). Although many writers of the Renaissance period, male and female alike, worked in a moment of transition from limited circulation of manuscript culture to the newly emerging public arena of print, for women to enter into the public arena through their writings was potentially a far more scandalous undertaking than it would have been for their male counterparts. Anne Bradstreet knew this. She watched as Anne Hutchinson, a member of her own church and community, was publicly humiliated for her intellectual intensity and independent thinking, resulting in her excommunication from the colony. Her reputation as a woman and mother was shattered. As John Winthrop fervently wrote in 1645, after leading the way to putting Hutchinson on trial:

> a godly young woman, and of special parts, who was fallen into a sad infirmity, the loss of her understanding, and reason, which had been growing upon her divers years, by occasion of her giving herself wholly to reading and writing, and written many books (XXX).

Bradstreet also would have heard her father and husband, both powerful figures in the colony, discuss the case against Hutchinson and how she was ultimately cast out of the community for stepping outside her prescribed role. Winthrop wrote:

> Mrs. Hutchinson, being removed to the Isle of Aquiday in the Narragansett Bay, after her time was fulfilled that she expected Deliverance of a child, was delivered of a monstrous child. (XXX)

Hutchinson, a prevailing leader of antinomianism, chose to speak out against the teachings of the Boston church. She held meetings in her home and wrote persuasive material counter to the accepted theology of the Puritans, which she distributed among her own coterie. In doing so, she was left in ruin. According to Winthrop and other intolerant members of the community, Hutchinson was punished by God, because it was believed that if you did not fulfill your natural duty, you would suffer God's wrath. The scholar Bronwen Price comments, "[T]he dominant cultural construction of women during the period in which feminine identity was linked to the female body and its status and, by association, female speech, especially in the public domain, was equated with sexual promiscuity" and sexual aberration (224). Thus, for entering into the public domain through reading and writing, neglecting her prescribed role as a Puritan woman, Hutchinson was punished for not being "good" and "godly" by bearing a "monstrous" child, a physical sign of female sexual promiscuity in seventeenth-century Puritan culture. Such promiscuity referred not only to sexual acts but extended even to thinking outside one's prescribed role as a woman. In order for Bradstreet to publicly express her views, she understood that she had to appear a godly woman or she, too, would be condemned by the cultural "elite" and possibly even by her own father.

Unlike Hutchinson, Bradstreet had two advantages: she was a member of upper-class society and she was well educated. Bradstreet implements these advantages in her own preface to *The Tenth Muse* to control the reader's perceptions of her as both "woman" and "author." The first stanza of "The Prologue," written with perfect lyrical precision, demonstrates Bradstreet's coy use of female modesty:

> To sing of Wars, of Captains, and of Kings,
> Of Cities founded, Commonwealths begun,
> For my mean pen are too superior things:
> Or how they all, or each their dates have run
> Let Poets and Historians set these forth,
> My obscure Lines shall not so dim their worth. (Ellis 100)

Bradstreet's first line, Virgilian in sound, boldly announces that she is setting out to write a history of English society, a feat historically only attempted by male poets from Homer to Milton. As soon as she asserts this lofty purpose, however, she immediately undermines herself by humbly downplaying her own writing, saying that her "mean" and "obscure" lines will not compare to poets of the past.

Although Bradstreet writes a perfect epic invocation, she just as quickly disclaims it. Her modesty continues in the second stanza as she comments on Du Bartas, a famous Puritan poet widely read by Puritans, that "A Bartas can do what a Bartas will / But simple I according to my skill" (Hensley 15). By stanza three, ironically continuing the perfect iambic pentameter and "abab" end rhyme of the earlier stanzas, Bradstreet invokes the Renaissance ideology of the "Great Chain of Being"; the stations into which people are born delineate their duties in society. While claiming to be a poet, a role considered unnatural for a woman, Bradstreet immediately underscores that ideology herself, writing:

> From Schoolboy's tongue no rhet'rick we expect,
> Nor yet a sweet Consort from broken strings,
> Nor perfect beauty where's a main defect:
> My foolish, broken, blemished Muse so sings,
> And this to mend, alas, no Art is able,
> 'Cause nature made it so irreparable. (Ellis 101)

By embracing the very ideology that constrains her instead of working against it as Hutchinson did, Bradstreet's seeming affirmation of the idea that by "nature" women are "blemished," "broken," and the weaker of the sexes, she appears to be upholding her role as woman, even though she is actually subverting it through the act of writing.

Bradstreet's tone, though seemingly modest, is increasingly sarcastic as she claims that she can't "cure" herself the way the great Greek orator Demosthenes conquered his speech defect, because "A weak or wounded brain admits no cure" (Ellis 101). If Bradstreet believed her own rhetoric about her ability to write and think as "defect," she would have seen producing *The Tenth Muse* as a futile act. Instead she attacks the rhetoric of critique, forecasting how critical members of her community, such as John Winthrop, may respond to her overstepping her bounds as a woman, as she writes:

> I am obnoxious to each carping tongue
> Who says my hand a needle better fits,
> A Poet's pen all scorn I should thus wrong,
> For such despite they cast on Female wits:
> If what I do prove well, it won't advance,
> They'l say it's stol'n, or else it was by chance. (Ellis 101)

As if directly speaking to a specific audience, Bradstreet rebuts the notion that her "hand a needle better fits," making it clear that she understands the gender politics of her position as a female "author." To advance her own ideas in writing, especially in print, because women supposedly are not "naturally" born with the "wit" to produce poetry, she acknowledges that she will be accused of stealing the ideas or that they were created "by chance." Later, in the prefatory dedication to her father, she makes it clear that "I honour him [Du Bartas], but dare not wear his wealth / My goods are true (though poor), I love no stealth." By claiming her "goods" Bradstreet appears to openly claim full responsibility for her work.

She continues in the next stanza, making the argument that it is not at all by "chance" that she can write, especially since there is already a tradition that affirms the female artist:

> But sure the Antique Greeks were far more mild
> Else of our Sexe, why feigned they those Nine
> And poesy made *Calliope's* own Child. (Ellis 101)

Inserting herself into a tradition that, as Bradstreet points out, was historically in the hands of women, the muses, Bradstreet uses the literary canon of her day to claim the authority to create as a female artist, hence the title of her book. She goes so far as to place herself in the direct lineage of the female. Mockingly she ends stanza 6, "But this weak knot they will full soon untie, / The Greeks did nought, but play the fools & lye" (Ellis 101).

Without specifying names, she uses the vague "they" to direct her comments to a specific audience that she knows will read her work and insulates herself from personal attacks through her evasiveness, similar to Odysseus's use of the Trojan horse to alter perception. This subtle gesture is an important move for Bradstreet because she implies that her critics will try to rationalize their thinking by rewriting history, calling the Greeks "fools" and liars. This glaring attack on her critics is not just about her reception but the kind of judgment all women face who claim the right to write. To keep women in their prescribed roles, maintaining the false notion that women by "nature" cannot contribute to public discourse, Bradstreet is aware of the desperate rationalizations used to keep women silent.

Bradstreet does not step outside her boundaries for long. Quickly parrying her own rhetoric, she seemingly submits once again: "Let Greeks be Greeks, and women what they are / Men have precedency and still excell"; it "vain" to try to "wage war" (Ellis 102). As quickly as she claims authority, she seems to submissively relent to the idea that her hand "a needle better fits," since "Men can do best, and women know it well." Yet, at the same moment Bradstreet seems to concede, her tone and the fact the she continues to write speak louder than the words on the page. Cunningly Bradstreet steps back into her role as dutiful woman, who is supposed to completely self-sacrifice to support husband, God, family, and society, to justify her writing by arguing to "men" that her "unrefined ore" will make "your glist'ring gold, but more to shine" (Ellis 102). Using self-deprecating metaphors, Bradstreet anticipates and appropriates her critics' rationalizations and most of all her own prescribed role, allowing her to write without appearing neglectful of her duties as a good Puritan woman.

II. FROM COTERIE TO PRINT:
THE PROMISCUITY OF PUBLIC EXCHANGE

Bradstreet's concerns as a female author in Puritan culture are twofold: how to write as a woman and how to circulate her words publicly without challenging her chastity. According to Psalm 51 of the Geneva Bible, when a woman promises God that if her sins are forgiven, "Then shal I teache thy waies unto the wicked, and sinners shal be converted unto thee" (51:13). A woman could circumvent cultural restrictions against female speech by presenting her words as godly service or, as in the case of Anne Bradstreet, presenting her words in the modest manner of a godly woman who remains faithful to her duties. Not unlike John Milton's intent to "justify God's way to man," Bradstreet states in her meditative prose, "I have not studied in this you read to show my skill, but to declare the truth, not to set forth myself, but the glory of God" (Bradstreet 25). As Bradstreet confronts the image of herself as a woman writer in *The Tenth Muse*, she must also contest the "promiscuous" image of public display, particularly print culture, which was considered a risky mode of discourse even for the male writer. For the Puritan man or woman, writing was always just on the edge of idolatry.

Bradstreet wrote during a critical juncture, where one system of production was beginning to circumvent another, a situation echoing our own movement from print to digital technology. Until the seventeenth century handwritten manuscripts were passed among a select social group. As Round describes:

> The poet's words entered a social circle known as a coterie, whose collaborative reading (and sometimes editing) of a text performed "the symbolic codes that designated rank" by nurturing a shared sense of taste among the assembled writer and readers. In the manuscript coterie, authorship was a civil or social space whose authority derived from the collective "poetics of exchange" set up by the circulation of the text in a select social circle, not from an individual and separate "author" in the modern sense of the word. (155)

Harold Love refers to manuscript culture as "scribal publication," where the writer was authorized by a collective group in which the *mano* (hand) *script* (text) was literally passed from hand to hand among a select social elite. Because it was so new, secular print seemed a dangerous endeavor because it "threatened to render manuscript circulation and the patronage network obsolete . . . publication made 'common' the flow of information that up to this time had been guarded within private channels." To counteract readers' distrust, printing had "to be imagined in ways that made it acceptable to audiences who understood and valued the text within the patronage system of manuscript exchange" (Wall 173). A vast array of strategies quickly became convention, as writers sought to legitimize their participation in a newer public print exchange.

In her study of English Renaissance male writers such as William Percy, Phillip Sidney, and Edmund Spenser, Wendy Wall examines the variety of such conventions to "explain" or "justify" printed texts. The most common means for a writer or printer "to ease the text in the public eye" was by suggesting that publication did not have full authorial consent, a strategy of dissociating text and author that created a skewed vision of printed texts since they seemed to be private words snatched away from their producers and offered for sale to the public (Wall 173). As Wall describes, "Discourse was written as private and secretive matter unveiled in a moment of transgression. Reading became figured as an act of trespass" (173). The corresponding metaphor of illicit sexuality extends beyond authorial reluctance as published books are portrayed as bodies lavishly displayed to a public audience. The pen becomes representative of the virgin, while the "press was branded a whore" as in Thomas Heywood's preface to *The Golden Age* (Wall 181). The sexualized language, explains Wall, ushers in the common metaphor of writing as reproduction as texts "undergo a pressing" and readers "ravish" the page; the maiden manuscript's chastity is victimized, producing illegitimate offspring (182-3). The printed text becomes the bastard child, an aberration of manuscript coterie.

Like her male contemporaries, Bradstreet emulates such manuscript coterie conventions in her prefatory gestures. Included before the official prologue to *The Tenth Muse* are eleven commendatory poems written by prominent men of society. Even Nathaniel Ward, author of the popular "The Simple Cobler of Aggawam in America" (written under the pseudonym Theodore de la Guard) and minister of Ipswitch where Anne and Simon Bradstreet, Thomas Dudley, and John Woodbridge resided, who chauvinistically commented on certain women's "squirrel brains," comments to the reader, "It half revives my chil frost-bitten blood, / To see a Woman once, do ought that's good" (Bradstreet 85). That the contributors and dedicatees are all male suggests a self-conscious fashioning, and their presence as prominent men lends an affirmation of the legitimacy of Bradstreet's work. These men assume responsibility for Bradstreet's appearance into print and uphold her image as a chaste, dutiful woman "honoured, and esteemed where she lives, for her gracious demeanor, her eminent parts, her pious conversation, her courteous disposition, her exact diligence in her place, and descrete managing of her family occasions."

The prefatory poems mimic the personae of a small, colonial family circle, where Bradstreet's "private" handwritten poems circulated as part of the very social act that constituted manuscript culture. This fashioning of "privacy," while legitimizing Bradstreet's work through manuscript mimicry, subverts the public reader's position and the position of the author herself. Reader becomes voyeur, "trespassing" on the private space of the manuscript coterie, reinforcing the metaphor of illicit sexuality. Bradstreet, the "discrete" proper woman, is betrayed at the hands of her own coterie, who "pressed" to reveal her writing publicly.

The metaphor extends further in the poem "The Author to Her Book," ironically appearing after the last poem, "The Vanity of All Worldly Things," in the 1678 posthumous edition of *The Tenth Muse*. Scholars such as John Ellis approximate the composition of "The Author to Her Book" around 1647, during Bradstreet's writing of the first edition (Bradstreet 88, 389). Why Bradstreet did not include the poem in the first edition remains a mystery. However, one can speculate that the climate in which the 1650 edition first appeared, only a few years after the Hutchinson trial and the incident

with her own sister, was not conducive to female expression. To claim any
authorship would have jeopardized her position as a young wife with a family. Plus, the inclusion of the poem in the first edition would have exposed as
false Bradstreet's and her brother-in law's claim that the book was published
without her consent. By 1678 the climate had shifted enough that Bradstreet
intended for the poem's inclusion in the second edition. On the title page of
this edition, titled *Several Poems*, it reads, "The Second Edition, Corrected
by the Author, and enlarged by an Addition of Several other Poems found
amongst her Papers after Death." This edition was printed in Boston by John
Foster. Clearly, Bradstreet no longer felt the social pressure to disregard her
role as author.

In "The Author to Her Book" the sexualized language is evident from the
beginning, as Bradstreet evokes the common convention among Renaissance
writers—the metaphor of reproduction. Claiming "authorship" Bradstreet
writes, "Thou ill-form'd offspring of my feeble brain, / Who after birth did'st
by my side remain" (Bradstreet 388). Once again her tone is self-deprecating
but also personal, that of a mother speaking to her child. While the metaphor
of reproduction is a common convention used among her male contemporaries, Bradstreet takes it one step further by making herself the narrator of
the poem, speaking as a "mother" to her "child," sacred images in Puritan
culture.

But, the child is an aberration, an "ill-form'd offspring." Bradstreet's text is
"snatched" by "friends" and "exposed to public view," like a body disrobed.
Referring to the kidnapers of her text as "friends" reinforces the image of privacy indicative of the coterie established in the prefatory dedications. What
is interesting is that all of her "friends" are male. Thus, Bradstreet is disrobed
by the very men who uphold her chastity. Forced to "press," Bradstreet's text
becomes "a rambling brat (in print) should a mother call" (Bradstreet 389).
The printed text becomes a bastard child, "unfit for light" with "blemishes"
and "defects." At the same time, Bradstreet once again evokes the image of
mother as she writes, "Yet being mine own, at length affection would / Thy
blemishes amend, if so I could" (Bradstreet 389). Here the corpus nature of
the text is personified even further, as she writes:

> I wash'd thy face, but more defects I saw,
> And rubbing off a spot still made a flaw.
> I stretcht thy joynts to make thee even feet,
> Yet still thou run'st more hobling then is meet. (389)

Bradstreet extends the metaphor of the poem as her child by using language
to personify the poem as a body, but the image of "joynts" and "feet" also
refers to the technical features of lyrical poetry, a poetic form often written

in iambic pentameter, with rhyming stanza patterns where "feet" measure the accented and unaccented syllables in a single line. Apologetic that she cannot provide "better dress," Bradstreet closes the poem by sending her "child" text "out of door" into the marketplace, warning:

> In this array, 'mongst Vulgars mayst thou roam
> In Criticks hands, beware thou dost not come,
> And take thy way where yet thou art not known,
> If for thy Father askt, say, thou hadst none:
> And for thy mother, she alas is poor,
> Which caus'd her thus to send thee out of door. (390)

Like a good mother, Bradstreet warns the child to stay away from the vulgarity associated with the marketplace, yet admits that the child by nature is illegitimate since it has no father. By claiming and flaunting responsibility for the text as a single mother who alone produced the offspring, Bradstreet takes full responsibility as author, undermining the claim she establishes in the beginning of the poem that it was her friends who "exposed" the text to public view. Bradstreet becomes the fallen woman who has succumbed to seduction, producing a child out of wedlock.

Yet, it is not the image of a fallen woman that the reader sees. Controlling the image, Bradstreet quickly forces the reader to see her instead as a good mother who warns her child about the "vulgar" world and as a poor victim forced by society, since she has no husband, to provide for herself by entering into the forbidden marketplace. Self-authorizing herself in such a way, Bradstreet justifies her "home-spun art" and daringly challenges her critics' sentiments about female authorship. The rhetoric of self-presentation takes on a broader aspect than the conventional language of authorial modesty. As Helen Wilcox explains:

> The topos of humility, when conventionally used by highly educated male authors, is not intended to highlight the author's weaknesses. The woman writer who asks for "pardon" for her "error" in writing, on the other hand, is drawing attention to her transgression against social and religious ideology as well as literary convention. However, the familiar trope of the reluctant author can play a vital role for the woman whose writing, if construed as deliberate, might be seen as a flouting of a woman's proper passivity (for which read also chastity and holiness). Thus the stress on the justification of women's writing on emotional grounds . . . is a further gendered feature of their self-construction. (214)

As a whole, then, Bradstreet's *Tenth Muse* demonstrates fully the logic of Renaissance author formation, especially for women, as coterie texts competed with and moved into the marketplace. The personification of her text and its mimicry of manuscript coterie circulation "grew out of her attempts to negotiate the civil boundaries that had been set up to guard male authorship against female encroachment," allowing her to move into the marketplace and become a participant in "the larger discourse surrounding female authorship in early modern English culture as a whole" (Round 156). More important, Bradstreet's method of self-authorship allowed her to negotiate her social agency and step out of her gendered role to become a participating member of civil discourse.

III. "TO PLAY THE REX"

Bradstreet's construction of her social agency in *The Tenth Muse* extends beyond the prefatory material. A major problem with much of Bradstreet scholarship is that it focuses on individual poems as autonomous artifacts, unrelated to each other. However, when one reads the text as a single body, not to be amputated by close readings of individual texts, *The Tenth Muse* reads like a political manifesto, similar to those of her male contemporaries, such as John Milton's *Aeropagitica*. As described by the scholar Eliza New, Bradstreet's work takes the form of "a colonial feminism that shunned militancy and embraced ministry—that, in fact, reserved its gravest suspicions for what we call 'politics'" (99). In fact, when Bradstreet's poetry arrived in the marketplace it was included in George Thomason's collection of tracts and pamphlets of the English Civil War (Round 156). While the newly emerging print culture mimicked the material nature of manuscript coterie, it also served the same social function. The discursive space of manuscript transmission "cloaked politics in speculative treatises on theology, petitions, depositions, personal and corporate histories, and even works of lyric poetry" (Round 169). As Philip Round describes, manuscripts were circulated in both British and colonial society to:

> hide "seditious" thought in times of oppression, to convey things dangerous to speak of in their own local culture of surveillance, and . . . in their conception of reading, the circulation of manuscripts was understood to be constitutive of a social order called the community of saints, whose roots were in the nuclear family. Manuscript writing offered New Englanders an outlet for ideas that might otherwise risk severe political censure if released into a print culture where punishment was harsh and swift. Even a powerful man like John Winthrop chose first to circulate his ideas about antinomianism in manuscript before publishing them to the world at the height of the Hutchinson controversy. (169)

The manuscript coterie made politics personal. The "private" setting of manuscript transmission produced emotionally charged "gestural politics of immediacy and veracity" usually associated with the face-to-face audience of the oral tradition. The reader becomes part of an intimate scribal community "as the familiarity of the script paralleled the intimacy of personal relations and the experience of being in the know as a confidant" (Round 170). The act of reading becomes a dichotomy. Reader is both voyeur, trespassing on the private space of the coterie, and "confidant," entrusted with the handwritten text and granted access to the political elite.

Printed text, "dressed" to reflect manuscript culture, was highly political and polemical, providing the ideal space for women because it appeared "private" and "familial." This is particularly important for Bradstreet. While female authorship was rapidly growing in England, with two hundred works printed from 1649 to 1688, Bradstreet's *Tenth Muse* remains the only printed text by a woman in the New World during the same era. Women who published works in England during the Interregnum enjoyed the social mobility created by the English Civil War, and the rapid expansion of urban spaces decreased rates of censure. Bradstreet, residing in the American colonies, felt the need to "dress" her text acceptably. Her response was directly related to the cultural climate of New England, since there was no space "that was not carefully surveyed by an activist clergy" (Round 173), especially for a woman wishing to express her political and religious views.

In 1638, the date of Bradstreet's elegy to Sir Philip Sidney, the earliest poem in *The Tenth Muse*, the political, religious, economic, and cultural differences within the Massachusetts Bay Colony were widening and threatening to fragment the infant commonwealth. The central figure of the antinomian controversy was Anne Hutchinson, a middle-aged woman who left England in 1634 to follow the much-admired Reverend John Cotton to the New World. Hutchinson was a prominent nurse-midwife and spiritual advisor to women in the new Massachusetts colony. Sometime during her first two years in Boston she began holding weekly gatherings for the purpose of reviewing and commenting on the sermon of the previous Sunday. The meetings were exclusively attended by women at first but quickly grew to include men. With a steady attendance of sixty or more of the town's inhabitants, including the young governor, Henry Vane, and a number of other men of power and prominence, Hutchinson's meetings evolved into more of a political quorum (Lang 4). Rather than recapitulating the weekly sermon, as a regular part of her critiques she reproached the Massachusetts clergy, accusing them of falling into a covenant of works. Hutchinson claimed that the clergy mistakenly took the Puritan theology of sanctification, the successful struggle of the soul against sin, as evidence of election. She felt they denied that works and redemption bear no necessary connection. Hutchinson and her supporters instead promoted a doctrine of free grace, characterized by the inefficacy of works and the absolute assurance of the saint. As Hutchinson's followers became increasingly convinced that the Massachusetts Bay ministers were guilty of preaching a covenant of works and claiming electoral power as self-elected saints, spiritual anxiety spread among the Boston parishioners, driving many of them to walk out of church meetings, decrying their spiritual leaders as "nobodies" (Round 110). Efforts were made to replace the Reverend John Wilson, pastor of the Boston church, where the Bradstreet attended. Hutchinson's followers wanted John Wheelwright, Hutchinson's brother-in-law, ordained as the new pastor of the Boston church.

By 1636 the ministers of Boston, along with other elite clerical parties, specifically the Reverend John Cotton, Nathaniel Ward of Ipswich, and Hugh Peter of Salem, heard the claims that Hutchinson not only held unendorsed meetings in her home but had begun "to disesteem generally the Elders of the churches" (Hall 384). Singling Hutchinson out as the source of the growing political and spiritual anxiety, she was questioned about matters of doctrine and ordinance. Animosity grew as accusations of antinomianism from the clerical elite were met with charges of papism from Hutchinson supporters. A flagrant attack by John Wheelright was delivered during the Fast Day, which was organized in an effort to restore peace in the fragmenting commonwealth. Wheelright's sermon directly attacked the spiritual organization of the colony, stating that New England's ministers preached a "covenant of works" doctrine, a code phrase for a religion lacking sufficient grace or "indwelling of the spirit" (Round 111).

Tensions mounted. By the fall of 1637 the General Court, in a stern and symbolic gesture, convicted Anne Hutchinson of sedition, banishing her and her own congregation from the colony. Hutchinson had overstepped her discursive role as a Puritan woman. Often called a "language controversy" by scholars, the Hutchinson case can be simplified as a case about censure. Acting as an outspoken, articulate member of society, Hutchinson threatened the power of central figures of clerical leadership. Thus, to quiet her "carping tongue," she was censured, banished, and called a witch for accessing, disseminating, and ultimately entering into the field of cultural production in a manner that was considered "the Misgovernment of [a] Woman's Tongue" (Hall 384). John Winthrop wrote on November 1, 1637:

> The court also sent for Mrs. Hutchinson, and charged her with divers matters, as her keeping two public lectures every week in her house, whereto sixty or eighty persons did usually resort, and for reproaching most of the ministers (viz., all except Mr. Cotton) for not preaching a covenant of free grace, and that they had not the seal of the spirit, nor were able ministers of the New Testament; which were clearly proved against her, though she sight to shift it off. And after many speeches to and fro, at last she was so full she could not contain, but vented her

revelations; amongst which this was one, that she had it revealed to her that she should come into New England, and she should her be persecuted, and that God would ruin us and out posterity and the whole state for the same. So the court proceeded and banished her. (XXX)

Hutchinson became the token "fallen" woman who committed heresy and sedition by refusing to submit to "lawful" authority and to play the part of "good" woman.

Such events in New England mirrored the tensions growing in Old England with the growing civil crisis. England was in a similar struggle regarding the centralization of power within the clerical elite, as reformers demanded that the autocratic power of the churchmen in office, elected by the king, be removed. Martin Luther's reformation had finally hit Old England full force as English reformers, among whom were John Milton and Bradstreet's own brother-in-law, John Woodbridge, began fighting the Church of England's power to censure and control civil discourse. Parliament formed the Committee on Religion, which recommended the expulsion of bishops from the House of Lords, a measure passed by the House of Commons and, after some delay, by the upper house. Angered, Charles I circumvented all the rights of the constitutional monarchy, arriving himself to arrest for high treason the offending members who were the prime organizers of reform. The king was met by a Parliament united against his censuring of their power, and a growing number of civilian supporters, similar to Hutchinson's supporters, sought to remove the king, marking the beginning of the English Civil War. The struggle of autocratic and theocratic power verses participatory government and the struggle for free speech uncensored by an "elected" clerical body thus reached across the ocean.

The macrocosmic events surrounding the antinomian crisis and the English Civil War registered on the microcosm of Anne Bradstreet's personal world as she describes the atmosphere as "a world turned upside down." As the gap between Old and New England widened between 1637 and 1647, Bradstreet's own family divided as they struggled with the growing strife that was festering both in their new homeland and their old country of origin. When Hutchinson was brought to trial before the General Court in November 1637, Simon Bradstreet was in attendance as an assistant along with Bradstreet's father, Thomas Dudley, who was also the deputy governor. By the 1638 church trial, Simon Bradstreet was not an attendee since he was not a minister, and he left his membership in the Boston church, having by this time relocated with Anne to Ipswich, a more liberal and tolerant community within the Massachusetts Bay Colony. Although there is no clear evidence that Simon Bradstreet was sympathetic to the antinomians, he is on record as stating he was not opposed to women's meetings and he thought that such meetings were "lawful" (Hall 327). It is clear, however, that Simon Bradstreet and his father-in-law did not share the same sentiments toward the Hutchinson case. While Dudley spoke openly against the antinomians, Simon Bradstreet favored a more balanced approach of tolerance.

No doubt the Dudley-Bradstreet family disagreements, symbolized through the Bradstreets' relocation to Ipswich, only escalated when in 1637 a letter to the Massachusetts magistrates arrived from England, "admonishing the young colony for allowing individual congregations an ever-tightening control over family life and the religious and political freedoms of its citizens" (Rosenmeir 82). The letter underscored the ties between Old and New England, accusing the magistrates of breaking with the original spirit of independence and with the international solidarity that English Puritans felt was an essential part of their movement (Rosenmeir 82). This letter fueled the civil unrest not only within the New England colony but also within the Dudley-Bradstreet family. It is clear in an autobiographical letter to her children that the uproar regarding these issues had an impact on Anne Bradstreet's faith. Bradstreet writes:

> [S]ome new Troubles I haue had since ye world has been filled wth Blasphemy, and Secretaries, and some who haust been acctd. sincere Xtians have been carried away wth them, that somt: I haue said, Is there Faith vpon ye Earth & I haue not known what to think, But then I haue Remebred the words of Christ that so it must bee, and that if it were Possible ye ver elext should be deceived. (28)

This is clearly a reference to Christ's chastising the Pharisees for being vain and pious about their "elect" positions. Bradstreet recognized the fallacy of the magistrates, who included her own father.

Tensions only increased from 1637 with the trial of Hutchinson to 1647 when Bradstreet's own sister was convicted of similar charges for "hir irregular Prophesying in mixt Assemblies and for Refusing ordinarily to Heare in ye Churches of Christ" (Ulrich 111). Anne Bradstreet was very close to her sister, having acted as her surrogate mother after their mother died, and having named her second daughter Sarah. Sarah had followed her husband, Benjamin Keayne, to England. When she arrived in London, Sarah was reported to have "'growne a great preacher'" (White 174). Through a series of events, Sarah's husband abandoned her, forcing her to return to Boston alone, where she immediately encountered charges reminiscent of the Hutchinson trial.

Thomas Dudley was once again governor; thus he served during the proceedings of the General Court during the trial of his own daughter. Unlike Simon and Anne Bradstreet, Dudley was an ardent opposer of toleration and did little to protect his own daughter. A poet himself, Dudley wrote on a scrap of paper, found in his pocket after his death in 1653:

> Let Men of God in Courts and Churches watch
> O're such as do a Toleration hatch,
> Lest that Ill Egg bring forth a Cockatrice,
> To poison all with Heresie and Vice.
> If Men be left, and otherwise Combine
> My Epitaph's, *I Dy'd no Libertine.* (Rosenmeir 91)

These last lines of a farewell poem to both his wife and children conclude startlingly with an admonition against "toleration," which was seen as a generative force in the commonwealth. Clearly the issue of toleration plagued Dudley to the day of his death, and his belief in anti-toleration was so unyielding that he condemned his own daughter. Dudley's use of "cockatrice" deliberately paints the picture of a woman who acts not as a good "mother hen" but instead as a female "cock." Dudley's poem reveals that toleration will only lead to "ill eggs" that "bring forth" women who overstep their roles. He concludes that such eggs should not be allowed to hatch. Thus, in 1647 Sarah was excommunicated by the Boston church for "irregular prophesying" and charged with "odius, lewd & scandalous uncleane behaviour" (White 176). Even as a contemporary reader it is easy to imagine Anne Bradstreet's horror when her own father not only excommunicated her sister from the community but disowned her.

What differed significantly between Hutchinson's trial and Sarah's is that Sarah's accusers provided no particulars of her crime, and she was given no chance to respond. The historian Laura Ulrich writes:

> The charge of "unclean behavior" . . . must be approached with great caution. Attacks upon religious dissenters frequently included charges of sexual irregularity, as though disruption on one social boundary inevitably entailed the disruption of another. It would be helpful to know what Sarah had been preaching in those assemblies. Puritan authority (both in England and Old) was continuously challenged from its own left flank by men and women who turned spirituality into a weapon for attacking the established order. The first church was still weeding out Anne Hutchinson's supporters when Sarah came as a young bride to Boston; ten years later the memory of Hutchinson's disruptive teaching still colored the churches response to female dissent. But without further evidence we can only speculate. (112)

Perhaps, as Ulrich suggests, Sarah did not listen or attend the right church regularly, but the fact that she was not allowed to verbally defend herself suggests that the New England Congregationalists increasingly worried about citizens speaking openly and freely, especially women. This could be attributed to the fear surrounding public censure in England, the disempowerment of elite leadership by the rising middle class, and the increased literacy of the masses, especially women. As the scholar Cheryl Walker describes, "[D]uring the 1640's and 1650's—when Bradstreet wrote most of her poems—there was an outpouring of especially virulent misogyny in the mother country" (3). Thus, to accuse Sarah Dudley of "irrational" behavior and of being "really unbalanced" may have had more to do with the misogynous lens through which the Puritan world, old and new, had come to view women who "prophesied" than with her actual verbal articulations and public discourse (White 174).

With the civic and religious battles hitting so close to home, Anne Bradstreet must have felt compelled to enter into the political conversation. Disturbed by the overly zealous censure of political and religious ideas that impacted even her own sister, Bradstreet's autobiographical letter suggests that she, like her husband, found toleration to be the reasonable position in the colony, in the homeland, and within her family. Bradstreet writes, "why may not ye popish Relign. Bee ye right, They haue the same God, the same Christ, ye same word, They only enterprett it one way wee another" (218). While the case against Hutchinson was disturbing, it was the horror of her own sister's trial that drove Bradstreet to publish *The Tenth Muse*, as evidenced by the date of publication (1650), only three years after Sarah's prosecution.

Bradstreet's statement of toleration, situated at the turbulent point in history when *The Tenth Muse* was published, provides the lens through which the body of her poetry should be read—as a political argument for tolerating diversity of thought and expression, especially for women who stepped out of their prescribed roles. Bradstreet creates the space to exert her politics of toleration by diffusing herself through the dramatically personified characters in the quaternions and by using the elegiac tributes to Sidney, Du Bartas, and Queen Elizabeth to uphold her social agency.

Immediately following the "Prologue" are Bradstreet's poems "The Elements," "The Humours," "The Ages of Man," and "The Four Seasons," for her "four times four" quaternions, which echoed a Hippocratic and Aristotelian scheme of things, indicative of Renaissance writers, who often reinvented Greek and Roman models and gave them a contemporary motif. Each poem consists of narrators, such as Water, Air, Fire, and Earth, who are connected to the characters in the proceeding poem through a type of family genealogy. Bradstreet writes, "Choler is owned by Fire, and Blood by Air, / Earth knew her black swarth child, Water her fair: / All having made obeisance by each mother" (33). All sixteen parts are personified like characters of a morality play as they take their places on the stage (Ellis xli).

It is important to note that although Puritans were not supportive of the theater—and in fact spoke actively against opening theater doors on the Lord's Day to crowds of "vagrant and lewd persons" who plagued and disturbed congregations with "raucous noise from drums and trumpets"—they

were influenced by theatrical culture (Adair 101). Puritans saw the theater
as an affront, especially since they had become the brunt of brutal jokes by
playwrights about their deviance from the English way of life, particularly
their extreme sobriety. Although the stage was not condoned by Puritans
in general, there were some who attended, especially Shakespeare's plays.
Counter to many playwrights, Shakespeare was a shrewd businessman who
wrote plays that appealed to a wider spectrum of people, including Protestants
and Puritans who could listen to his plays without offense since some of his
characters reflected Puritan values. Because of his ability to reach a wide
audience, Shakespeare's work was a major part of mass culture. Elizabethan
theater was so deeply woven into seventeenth-century English culture that
even Puritans could not avoid its influence.

Although a Puritan, Bradstreet would have been aware of common
dramatic techniques and the safe discursive space that creating characters
through which she could expound her politics would provide her. Beginning
immediately in the first poem, each of the four elements is chiefly interested
in telling how he is "the strongest, noblest and the best," exaggerating his
own virtues, if necessary, at the expense of the others (Bradstreet 103). Each
of the elements originally sets out to expound his own virtues and show how
his virtues benefit mankind. Good intentions are soon forgotten among the
four elements as each becomes interested only in his own seemingly important purpose, bragging:

> Who was of greatest use and might'est force;
> In placide terms they thought now to discourse,
> That in due order each her turn should speak;
> But enmity this amity did break
> All would be cheife, and all scorn'd to be under,
> Whence issu'd raines & windes, lightning, thunder. (Bradstreet 103)

Because of their own vanity, their "enmity this amity did break," leaving their
friendship ultimately destroyed by their own unwillingness to accept and see
the benefit of the other elements' difference.

Fire is the first to be personified, rhetorically asking, "What is my worth,
(both ye) and all men know," (Bradstreet 104). Fire answers her own question,
"The benefit all living by me find," and provides evidence for her assertion
of her own worth. Continuing, Fire begins listing the various ways in which
humans use fire, citing examples such as forging weapons, fashioning tools to
"subdue the Earth," making kitchen implements for cooking the "dayly food I
wholesome make," and for warming "shrinking Limbs" (Bradstreet 105). Fire
even vainly claims the position of deity, stating, "My planets of both Sexes
whose degree / Poor Heathen judg'd worthy a Deity," and then lists all the

important constellations that would not exist in such abundance without her flame (Bradstreet 106). Her claim to godliness continues: "Of old when Sacrifices were Divine, / I of acceptance was the holy signe" (Bradstreet 108). Fire then describes how, like a god, she can bring down entire civilizations and cities such as "*Ninus'* great wall'd town, & *Troy . . . Carthage*, and hundred more in stories told" into "confused heaps of ashes" (Bradstreet 107). Concluding her long list of justifications for having the most worth, Fire ends, "And then because no matter more for fire" (Bradstreet 108).

Not to be outdone by Fire, Earth argues:

> Sister (quoth shee) I come not short of you,
> In wealth and use I do surpass you all,
> And mother earth of old men did me call:
> Such is my fruitfulness, an Epithite,
> Which none ere gave, or you could claim of right,
> Among my praises this I count not least,
> I am th' original of man and beast. (Bradstreet 109)

Earth proceeds to brag about the "sundry fruits" she yields for mankind, claiming that man could not have built great civilizations without the land, animals, and other resources she provides. The other elements are inferior according to Earth because they cannot exist without her. Earth points out that Water would not be able to be contained without the land that she provides, and "Well knowest my fuel must maintain thy fire" (Bradstreet 111). She further undermines the benefits of the other elements, stating that all the "commodities" men utilize are because of Earth, as she reminds, "But Mariners where got you ships and Sails, / And Oars to row, when both my Sisters sails?" (Bradstreet 111). Purposefully echoing scripture, Earth concludes, "Remember Sons, your mould is of my dust / And after death whether interr'd or burn'd / As Earth at first so into Earth return'd" (Bradstreet 114). Earth ends her argument for being the most worthy by stating that all things come from her, even the other elements, and all things eventually return to her after death.

The final two elements make equally boastful claims in their soliloquies about their own worthiness. Water responds to Earth:

> Sister (quoth she) it had full well behoved
> Among your boastings to have praised me,
> Cause of your fruitfulness, as you shall see:
> This your neglect shows your ingratitude
> And how your subtilty would men delude. (Bradstreet 114)

Water acknowledges the praises of Earth, but the tone is sarcastic, as Water undercuts those praises by stating that Earth is deceptive. Water pronounces to Earth that she is bound to Water, not Water to Earth, because "Who am I thy drink, thy blood, thy sap and best: / If I withhold, what art thou? dead dry lump / Thou bearst no grass or plant nor tree, nor stump" (Bradstreet 114). Once again, Water lists the many ways in which she sustains mankind, the centuries of civilizations, and all the animals, providing the sustenance for Earth's resources.

> Air's argument in turn also boastfully claims superiority:
> I do suppose you'll yield without control
> I am the breath of every living soul.
> Mortals, what one of you that loves not me
> Abundantly more than my Sisters three?
> And though you love Fire, Earth and Water well
> Yet Air beyond all these you know t' excel. (Bradstreet 119)

After listing all the ways in which Earth could not sustain life without Air, Air asserts:

> I grow more pure and pure as I mount higher,
> And when I'm thoroughly rarifi'd turn to fire:
> And when I am condens'd, I turn to water,
> Which may be done by holding down my vapour.
> Thus I another body can assume,
> And in a trice my own nature resume. (Bradstreet 120)

Air becomes almost holy, symbolically becoming the three in one, an image in Christianity and in the Puritan culture of God.

What truly makes Air great, unlike the other three elements, is that Air acknowledges that they are all needed in order to benefit man:

> I have said less than did my Sisters three,
> But what's their wrath or force, the same's in me.
> To adde to all I've said was my intent,
> But dare not go beyond my Element. (Bradstreet 122)

Ultimately, Air attacks the other three elements' vanity in boasting their superior existence without acknowledging how the relationship between the elements is essential for any of them to survive. While beneficial to man, if unrestrained, each element can cause destruction. "Fire can turn a town to cinders; Earth, though productive, can bring famine and earthquake; Water, by its abundance or lack of it, can bring benefits or disaster; Air is the breath of every living thing without which it perishes" (Piercy 43). Thus, Air shows how they all commit the sin of vainly believing that each one is more important than the other and that they all instead should tolerate one another since they are so reliant on each other's differences.

The arguments of these four are not nearly as heated or as spiteful as those of the characters in the next poem, "The Four Humours." As with the four elements, the fault of the four humours lies in that each wishes to be chief, but the splenetic language escalates as each desires to be paramount even if it means slandering the others to do so. As the scholar Josephine Piercy notes, "Their arguments have the tone of political backbiting. There seems to be something more than the mere personification of man's humours" (43). The politics, however, seem gender related, as Choler becomes male, while the other three remain female.

The chiding among the four characters begins in the prologue to the poem:

> Choler first hotly claim'd right by her mother,
> Who had precedency of all the other;
> But Sanguine did disdain what she requir'd,
> Pleading her self was most of all desir'd.
> Proud Melancholy, more envious than the rest,
> The second, third, or last could not digest.
> . . . .
> Mild Felgm did not contest for chiefest place,
> Only she crav'd to have a vacant space.
> Well, thus they parle and chide; but to be brief,
> Or will they, nill they, Choler will be chief. (Bradstreet 122)

Choler is the first to take the stage, "To show my high descent and pedigree." Choler's unusually nasty attacks on the other humours reveal him to be an irascible figure as he calls them "milksops." Blood, "[w]hile worth the other two," is described as committing the sin of sloth, a trait not admired by the hardworking Puritans:

> Here's sister ruddy, worth the other two,
> Who much will talk, but little dares she do,
> Unless to Court and claw, to dice and drink,
> And there she will out-bid us all, I think,
> She loves a fiddle better then a drum. (Bradstreet 125)

Choler tells the reader that Blood enjoys attending court, gambling, and drinking. The image of a fiddle verses a drum reinforces the notion that Blood loves to "dice and drink" since fiddling is associated with dancing, while the "drum" is associated with marching and work. Choler's character seems suspiciously like a portrait of a British or colonial contemporary of Bradstreet's. Melancholy is described with equal scorn:

> Then here's our sad black Sister, worse than you,
> She'l neither say she wil, nor wil she doe;
> But peevish, Malecontent, musing sits,
> And by misprissons, like to loose her witts:
> If great persuasions cause her to meet her foe,
> In dull resolution she's so slow. (Bradstreet 126)

Melancholy is attributed with the traits indicative of a dim-witted woman who does not perform her duties. In fact, "misprisson" is by definition the neglect of duty by a public official. Phlegm is also described as a dim-witted woman by Choler:

> So loving unto all, she scornes to fight.
> If any threaten her, she'l in a trice,
> Convert from water to congealed ice:
> . . . .
> She dare not challenge if I speake amisse,
> Nor hath she wit, or heat, to blush at this. (Bradstreet 126)

Incapable of speaking up for herself, Phlegm becomes the helpless woman who cannot speak her mind.

The derogatory characterizations continue in Choler's soliloquy as he launches into a long anatomical analysis showing how all the other humours, with their "seats" in the human system, cannot function without him since he is the "heat": "Take Choler from a Prince, what is he more, / Then a dead Lyon?" Melancholy is especially ridiculed by Choler, with her seat in the spleen, as Choler chides, "So base thou art, that baser cannot be, / Th' excrement adustion of me" (Bradstreet 128). The attack on gender returns in the end as Choler claims, "And yet to make my greatness, still more great / What differences, the Sex? but only heat" (Bradstreet 128). Choler's final conclusion is that since he is male and has more "heat," he is superior to the other three "feminine" humours whose "foolish" brains are "wanteth" of heat.

Blood's braggadocio and snide comments only heighten the disdain among the humours as Phlegm is described as possessing "cruel art," Choler is the "most malignant," and Melancholy "seizes on man, with her uncheerful visage" (Bradstreet 130). Biding her time until Blood has refuted the slanderous remarks about her and has established her rightful place of importance, "Melancholy launches into a scathing diatribe against Choler:

> And so art call'd black Choler or adust;
> Thou witless think'st that I am thy excretion,
> So mean thou art in Art as in discretion:
> But by your leave, I'le let your greatnesse see;

> What Officer thou art to us all three.
> The Kitchen Drudge, the cleanser of the sinks,
> That casts out all that man e're eats, or drinks:
> If any doubt the truth whence this should come,
> Show them they passage to the' *Duodenum.*
> Thy biting quality still irritates,
> Till filth and thee nature exonerates. (Bradstreet 140)

Melancholy's anger and disdain for Choler only exaggerate the lack of toleration among the four humours of each other's difference, yet Phlegm, like her mother, Air, concludes with a unpredictable turn in the poem's tone—to settle their differences and unite. While she claims for herself the noblest parts of man, the Brain and the Soul, she argues that they should work together in harmony or otherwise all will fall into confusion:

> Let's now be friends; its time our spight was spent,
> Lest we too late, this rahnesse do repent,
> Such premises wil force a sad conclusion,
> Unlesse we 'gree, all fals into confusion.
> Let Sanguine, with her hot hand Choler hold,
> To take her moyst, my moistnesse wil be bold;
> My cold, cold Melanshollies hand shall clasp;
> Her dry, dry Cholers other hand shal grasp;
> Two hot, two moist, two cold, two dry here be,
> A golden Ring, the Posey, *Unity.* (Bradstreet 146)

Only when they work together, understanding and tolerating each other, will they be able to achieve "unity" and "amity."

The final two poems in the quaternion shift in tone as the characters in "Four Ages of Man" and "The Four Seasons" relate their tales. The spitefulness and the contention for supremacy of their elders in the previous two poems is replaced with each character's reflecting on his weaknesses and strengths. Through their frank observations of themselves they realize that neither outdoes another, and each character becomes symbolic of a larger whole; it takes all the ages to make one life and it takes all the seasons to make one year, as Old Age comments, "That he was young before he grew so old" (Bradstreet 147). After both Childhood and Youth lament about their qualities, Youth concludes, "Childhood and Youth are vain yea vanity" (Bradstreet 156). For the duration of the poem, the theme of excessive vanity is repeated by each of the ages. Vanity, synonymous with pride, is one of the seven deadly sins, which can lead men to fall from grace. As the reader moves from the previous quaternions to the ages and seasons, there seems to be a very definite progression, as if all the poems build upon one another, leading to the final conclusion that excessive vanity can destroy unity by its sheer intolerance of difference.

The symbolic connection that all the ages are part of a unified whole becomes further evident in the beginning of Middle Age's soliloquy, as he states:

> Childhood and Youth (forgot) I've sometimes seen
> And now am grown more staid who have bin green
> What they have done, the same was done by me,
> As was their praise or shame, so mine must be. (Bradstreet 156)

Middle Age ends with another comment on the pridefulness of men: "Man at his best estate is vanity" (Bradstreet 161). The last to enter the stage and speak is Old Age, who pays homage to the previous ages:

> What you have been, ev'n such have I before
> And all you say, say I, and somewhat more.
> Babe's innocence, youth's wilderness I have seen,
> And in perplexed Middle Age have been;
> Sickness, dangers, and anxieties have past,
> And on this state am come to act my last.
> I have been young, and strong and wise as you. (Bradstreet 161)

Old Age reflects on the past ages, commenting, "In every age I've found much vanity" (162). With the wisdom that can only come from living, like a message from a parable, Old Age tells the reader that it is not one's worldly possessions, "learning, rhetoric, wit so large," nor the power or "goodly state," but "what I have done well, that is my prop." Old Age continues, "He that in youth is godly, wise, and sage, / Provides a staff then to support his age" (162).

Old Age wisely relays Bradstreet's central message of the quaternions—a person's vanity leads to intolerance and corruption since, "From king to beggar, all degrees shall find / But vanity, vexation of the mind" (Bradstreet 167; Eccli. xii 1-8). Thus it is important to be tolerant of each other's differences, since all, like the characters in the quaternions, are part of a unified whole. Ironically, although Bradstreet is arguing for tolerance, she knows that as a woman writing in an extremely intolerant political and religious climate she must be careful about how she constructs her authorial voice in order to avoid censure and the possibility of being excommunicated by her own community (or by her father) for self-expression.

The various characters Bradstreet creates allow her to "dress" her message, diffusing her own gender, since the reader interacts with the voice of the character and not Bradstreet directly. By establishing characters in the quaternion that speak as if they are standing on a stage, Bradstreet is able to "play the rex," to borrow a phrase from her elegy on Queen Elizabeth. The best example of Bradstreet's "cloaking" herself in a male persona occurs in the final speech of the "Four Ages of Man," where Old Age is constructed as a male figure speaking to his audience. When Old Age describes his outward appearance, the audience sees a gray-haired man remembering the strong young man he used to be:

> My arms and hands once strong have lost their might;
> I cannot labour, much less can I fight.
> My comely legs as nimble, as the Roe
> My heart sometimes as fierce as Lion bold,
> Now trembling is, all fearful sad and cold. (Bradstreet 166)

It is this old man that the reader sees on the stage, not the young woman who is really beneath the costume. When the character professes, "We old men love to tell what's done in youth," it is a male voice, not a female one, the reader hears. As a wise older male member of the community, Old Age is able to tell the other characters and, most important, the reader the controversial message that everyone is too full of vanity and instead needs to be more tolerant—a revolutionary idea in both Old and New England.

This cross-dressing allows Bradstreet to "play" the rex; she is able "play" or act as a man who can speak openly in public. Also, by "dressing" as a male persona she is able to "play" the reader by controlling the reader's perspective. As when she and her brother-in-law claimed that she was not responsible for the publication of her text, by using a male character to voice her political and religious views Bradstreet removes herself from possible condemnation since she can claim that she is not really the one who spoke the words.

Bradstreet further removes herself from the characters she has created in the quaternions by contrasting their voices with her own. At the end of the four pieces, tacked on as if an afterthought, Bradstreet suddenly appears on the stage as herself:

> My Subjects bare, my Brain is bad,
> Or better Lines you should have had:
> The first fell in so naturally,
> I knew not how to pass it by;
> The last, though bad I could not mend,
> Accept therefore of what is penn'd,
> And all the faults that you shall spy
> Shall at your feet for pardon cry. (Bradstreet 180)

The pun on "bare" is no mistake, as Bradstreet purposefully "bares" herself before her audience, reminding the reader in the same self-deprecating tone she used in the prologue that she is just a woman.

Bradstreet borrows from Elizabethan theater to construct her authorial self, but she also borrows from the Renaissance elegiac tradition. Using this tradition to sing her praises of three figures she admired, Sidney, Du Bartas, and Queen Elizabeth, Bradstreet builds her own monumentality as an author by immortalizing these great public figures in poetry. A typical motif in Renaissance poetry, used by famous writers such as Shakespeare, Spenser, and even Sidney, the process of eulogizing a famous public figure not only secures the fame of the one being remembered through poetry but also secures publicly the fame of the one writing the eulogy. Again, it is no accident that the three figures Bradstreet chooses to eulogize are two poets whom she admired and who influenced her work, but also Queen Elizabeth. These three figures serve as examples justifying to the reader, as a type of rhetorical argument by the very nature of their public lives, Bradstreet's legitimacy as a writer. Sidney, a renowned man of "Arms and Arts," was one of the first writers to solidify his fame through the printed text. Du Bartas was also a well-known poet, especially popular among Puritan readers, who often referenced and used Elizabethan theatrical techniques in his writings. Finally, Bradstreet pays tribute to Queen Elizabeth, who glorified the "female sex" and "play[ed] the Rex" (Bradstreet 359).

Retaining the rhyming couplets associated with the elegiac tradition, Bradstreet begins paying tribute to Sidney's skill as a writer, as she uses a collage of conventional references:

> *Mars* and *Minerva* did in one agree,
> Of Arms and Arts he should a pattern be,
> *Calliope* and *Terpischore* did sing,
> Of Poesie, and of musick, he was King;
> His Rhetorick struck Polimnia dead,
> His Eloquence made *Mercury* wax red. (Bradstreet 345)

Bradstreet praises Sidney's very public and deep love for his country. As she acknowledges Sidney's loyalty, she links herself to him: "Then let none disallow of these my strains / Whilst English blood yet runs within my veins" (Bradstreet 347). Bradstreet links herself and her writing directly to Sidney through the bloodline they share as British citizens. At the same time she quickly undermines it by stating, "The more I say, the more they worth I stain, / They fame and praise is far beyond my strain" (347). Bradstreet is sure not to overstep her boundaries as a female poet, making certain the reader knows that she is inferior to Sidney, "The brave refiner of our British tongue" (347). After her brief interjection about the quality of her eulogizing, Bradstreet continues her tribute to Sidney's skill, using figures from Homer's *Iliad*. Sidney is raised to an almost mythical quality: "Though Sidney died his valiant name should live; / And live it doth in spite of death, through fame," since in "sad sweet verse" he is immortalized (348).

By recalling Sidney's fame in poetry, Bradstreet makes herself the orator who in turn secures her own fame in public verse. Toward the end, the poem's focus shifts from elegizing Sidney to reflecting on the quality of Bradstreet's own verse and fame:

> But *Sidneys* Muse can sing his worthiness.
> The Muses aid I crav'd, they had no will
> To give to their Detractor any quill;
> With high disdain, they said they gave no more,
> Since Sidney had exhausted all their store.
> They took from me the scribbling pen I had,
> (I to be eased of such a task was glad). (Bradstreet 350)

The muses become responsible for Sidney's fame since they control who holds the "scribbling pen"; Bradstreet once again shifts the focus of authorship from herself to the muses who "threw me my pen" (351). She secures her own social agency by elegizing Sidney, one of England's greatest poets, but at the same time she diffuses her role as author, "So Sidneys fame I leave to Englands rolls, / His bones do lie interr'd in stately Pauls" (351).

The elegy to Du Bartas is more private in tone, as Bradstreet begins with language more representative of a woman whose infatuations go beyond public admiration. Bradstreet speaks to her "Great, dear, sweet *Bartas*," relaying to him that "My ravish'd eyes and heart with faltering tongue, / In humble wise have vow'd their service long" (Bradstreet 353). Taken over by the strength of his lines, Bradstreet writes, "My dazled sight of late review'd thy lines, / Where Art, and more then art, in nature shines; / Reflection from their beaming Altitude / Did thaw my frozen hearts ingratitude" (353). The language paints an image of a woman speaking to her lover, an image that serves as a metaphor for her appreciation of his contribution to her skill as a writer. Bradstreet describes the process of reading Du Bartas, saying:

> But barren I my Dasey here do bring,
> A homely flower in this my latter Spring,
> If Summer or my Autumn age do yield
> Flours, fruits, in Garden, Orchard, or in Field,
> They shall be consecrated in my Verse,
> And prostrate offered at great *Bartas* Herse;
> My muse unto a Child I may compare. (Bradstreet 354)

Using the metaphor of a barren woman who unexpectedly becomes "abound" with flowers and "fruits" because of Du Bartas's "rays" that thaw the "frozen" ground, Du Bartas becomes a father to her muse, inspiring her to write. Yet the muse, like a child, "understanding lacks,"; she is a "silly prattler" who "speaks no words of sense" (354). This sexualized language of Bradstreet's reading experience and Du Bartas's influence on her places Du Bartas in the role of "father" of her poetry.

By placing Du Bartas in a role also associated with "husband" and "provider," Bradstreet is able to maintain her role as subservient woman. Her role as a woman, incapable of creating such "matchless" art, is further developed:

> Thus weak brain'd I, reading thy lofty stile,
> Thy profound learning, viewing other while,
> Thy Art in natural Philosophy,
> Thy Saint like mind in grave Divinity,
> Thy piercing skill in high Astronomy,
> And curious insight in Anatomy,
> Thy Physick, musick, and state policy,
> Valour in warr, in peace good husbandry.
> Sure lib'ral Nature did with Art not small,
> In all the arts make thee most liberal. (Bradstreet 354)

The repetition of the pronoun "thy" creates a kind of blazon, a technique often used in sonnets when a poet is cataloguing a lover's attributes. Here Bradstreet lists the traits she admires in Du Bartas, beginning by first undermining her own abilities as a writer and thinker, calling herself "weak brain'd." Bradstreet then tells the reader of Du Bartas's glory as a poet and how his fame spread from France to England, where "Thy fame is spread as far, I dare be bold, / In all the Zones, the temp'rate, hot, and cold" (355). As the poem ends, Bradstreet makes it clear that "Thy sacred works are not for imitation, / But Monuments to future Admiration," and that his fame shall "last while starrs do stand." Concluding with the same self-deprecating tone about her skills as a writer as she did in ending Sidney's elegy, Bradstreet writes, "I'le leave thy praise to those shall do thee right, / Good will, not skill, did cause me bring my Mite" (356). Through Bradstreet's eulogy Du Bartas is rescued from death by living through his "Fame" secured in her verse. Since Bradstreet is responsible for securing his monumentality as a writer, even though she subverts her responsibility by stating that she was impregnated by Du Bartas's inspiration, Bradstreet's own authority is secured. The public gesture of securing Du Bartas's fame in verse gives legitimacy to Bradstreet as the poet who revives him in verse.

Although Queen Elizabeth died before Anne Bradstreet was born, the tales of the great sovereign whom her father once served in the war against Philip

II of Spain must have nurtured Bradstreet's imagination. Like the previous elegies, this tribute to the queen departs from the narrative manner of the quaternions and follows much more closely the traditional elegiac form of rhyming couplets. Unlike the other two elegies, however, this follows the form much more formally, containing the usual three parts, if the reader considers the two final epitaphs as one part. "The Proeme" pays tribute to one just dead; "The Poem" recounts the queen's accomplishments; "The Epitaph," especially the second piece, rejoices in the sovereign's undying fame (Piercy 67). "The Poem" is the most interesting, since Bradstreet pays tribute not only to Queen Elizabeth the ruling monarch, but to Queen Elizabeth who glorified the "female sex" and "wip'd off th' aspersion . . . that women wisdome lack to play the Rex" (Bradstreet 359). Bradstreet begins by praising the queen:

> No Phoenix pen, nor Spencers poetry,
> No Speeds nore Camdens learned history,
> Elizahs works, warrs, praise, can e're compact;
> The World's the Theatre where she did act.
> No memoryes or volumes can contain
> The 'leven Olympiads of her happy reign.
> Who was so good, so just, so learn'd, so wise,
> From all the Kings on earth she won the prize. (358)

Bradstreet's adoration is clearly apparent, and she uses the reference to the Renaissance theater, of which the queen herself was so fond. The word "act" has a double meaning, referring to the queen as one who "dressed" the part for the stage as an actor and as one who causes action. Already within these first few lines, Bradstreet depicts the queen as a leader, in control, rising above other "kings" because of her skills, brains, and wisdom. Through the elegiac praises the reader is led straight into Bradstreet's argument that woman can "play the rex."

To support her claim regarding the "female sex," she begins listing, or rather cataloguing, Queen Elizabeth's accomplishments and praises her as an earthly Minerva. Of great monarchs, "Millions will testify that this is true," that this queen was one of the greatest. And, among great women, this queen becomes the exceptional example. Bradstreet lists her above Semiramis, Tomris, Dido, Cleopatra, Zenobya, and all the rest, since the queen has "no fit parallel" (Bradstreet 360). Bradstreet is not only piling up evidence that Queen Elizabeth was a great leader, but because she was a woman, she becomes an example of the greatness of the "female sex." Elizabeth herself is "argument enough to make you mute" (Bradstreet 359). The pronoun "You," a personal reference to her reader, leads one to suspect that Bradstreet had a specific readership in mind, and she could have been speaking directly to those who would try to censure her work because they only saw her as a scribbling woman. In fact, Bradstreet practically names the individuals to whom she is directing her argument:

> Now say, have women worth? or have they none?
> Or had they some, but with out Queen is't gone?
> Nay Masculines, you have thus taxt us long,
> But she, though dead, will vindicate our wrong.
> Let such as say our sex is void of reason,
> Know 'tis a Slander now but once was Treason. (361)

Bradstreet boldly attacks the very idea that women are incapable of "reason," a statement repeated among members of her own community, such as John Winthrop during the trials of Anne Hutchinson and Sarah Dudley. And, if Bradstreet is writing in direct response to her father's actions against her sister, Bradstreet is ultimately accusing her father of "treason" not just against Queen Elizabeth but against the family.

In the third part of the elegy, "The Epitaph," Bradstreet uses a similar maneuver as she did in the first two elegies. Bradstreet gains social agency by being the author who publicly secures Queen Elizabeth's fame:

> *Here lyes the pride of Queens, Pattern of Kings,*
> *So blaze it, Fame, here's feathers for thy wings.*
> *Here lyes the envi'd, yet unparalleled Prince,*
> *Whose living virtues speak (though dead long since).*
> *In many worlds, as that Fantastick fram'd,*
> *In every one be her great glory fam'd.* (362)

The first line of the epitaph refers to the great sovereign among both "queens" and "kings." Queen Elizabeth is not relegated to a single gendered role as a sovereign; she surmounts both. Bradstreet especially plays with social constructions by calling the queen an "unparalleled prince." This implies an earlier description where Bradstreet describes the queen as acting on a stage. Like Bradstreet who fluctuates between female and male speakers in the quaternions, using the various personae to create a position of authority that would be accepted by her reader, so does Queen Elizabeth as she moved between acting both genders as her monarchy demanded.

Though Queen Elizabeth becomes the example by which Bradstreet models her own role as a public figure who must carefully negotiate the boundaries of her gender, Elizabeth also becomes the foundation of Bradstreet's social agency. Once again, because Bradstreet is the codifier of Elizabeth's fame, Bradstreet's position is secured by the public act of remembering England's great queen.

IV. VEXED BY VANITY, SHE SPEAKS HER MIND

The Tenth Muse concludes with the poem "The Vanity of All Worldly Things." The final poem serves as the summation of Bradstreet's central argument—that humankind can have too much "vanity" or pride, thus leading to the inability to tolerate difference. Bradstreet's use of theatrical personae in the quaternions and her use of the elegiac form to gain authority and social agency become the foundation upon which she makes her final public decry of censure. Echoing the biblical phrases "Him without sin, cast the first stone" and "Judge not lest yea be judged," Bradstreet clearly states to the reader that those who think they are without vanity are the worst offenders since they are so prideful in thinking that they are superior to everyone else. The narrator explains, "As he said vanity, so vain say I / Oh! vanity, O vain all under Sky," beginning the poem with the image of a man passing judgment on possessing vanity, yet the narrator comments that he is just as vain; in fact, everyone is vain and there is no man who possesses a "Consolation sound" (386). The narrator reminds readers that no one is above anyone else; no one is exempt from death or the turn of fate:

> No, they like Beasts and Sons of men shall dye:
> And whil'st they live, how oft doth turn their fate;
> He's now a captive, that was King of late.
> What is't in wealth great Treasures to obtain?
> No, that's but labour, anxious care, and pain,
> He heaps up riches, and he heaps up sorrow,
> It's his to day, but who's his heir to morrow? (Ellis 386)

As the narrator continues to attack the nature of individuals who possess too much vanity, the argument relates back to the images in the quaternions, reinforcing the central theme prevalent throughout *The Tenth Muse*. Reminiscent of the "Four Ages of Man," the narrator repeats:

> What is't in flowring youth, or manly age?
> The first is prone to vice, the last to rage.
> Where is it then, in wisdom, learning arts?
> Sure if on earth, it must be in those parts:
> Yet these the wisest man of men did find
> But vanity, vexation of mind. (Ellis 387)

The straightforward, polemical, and didactic tone questions whether anyone is free from committing the vice of vanity. The repetition of "But vanity, vexation of mind," a quote in Old Age's soliloquy as well, reinforces the foundation of Bradstreet's argument that even the "wisest" of men are vexed by too much pride, which hinders their judgment of fellow citizens and even their own family.

Questioning, in the tone of a personal religious meditation, the narrator wonders, "Where shall I climb, sound, seek, search, or find / That *summum bonum* which may stay my mind," searching for someone to provide an adequate example of one who has not been tainted by the power of vanity. The question is answered through the example of Christ, "the living crystal fount." Only those who choose to follow "this pearl of price, this tree of life, this spring," will overcome the "death" and "destruction" of worldly fame (Bradstreet 388). For Bradstreet, her answer lies in her devout Puritan faith: only Christ "satiates the soul" and "stays the mind" whereas "And all the rest, but vanity we find" (388). Since none can follow the perfect example of Christ, no one has the right to pass judgment and be intolerant of political or religious difference.

Vexed by the vanity she sees turning her world "upside down" because of individuals' claiming unauthorized religious and political power, Bradstreet sets out to speak her mind. Although there is little hard evidence for this, other than the internal gestures provided in the material nature of the manuscript, particularly the prefatory responses, Bradstreet's message ultimately extends beyond the traditional coterie. Entering into the metropolis from manuscript to print, Bradstreet's verse collection accrues new meaning by acting on and responding to the local along with transatlantic conversations regarding antinomianism and individuals' right to participate in civil discourse. Ironically, for Bradstreet to participate in civic conversations as a woman writer she had to carefully and deliberately create a discursive space that would not jeopardize her position as a dutiful mother and wife, while affording herself the right to write. By controlling the material production of the text during a time of rapid transition from manuscript coterie to mass printing distribution, along with her own presence as author and speaker within the text, Bradstreet transcended her role as a Puritan woman, becoming instead a public reformer who argued for political and religious toleration. And through her carefully constructed authorial presence and social agency within a male-dominated field of literary production, Bradstreet set the stage for future writers, especially women.

Chapter Two

Phillis Wheatley: She Must "be refin'd, and join th'angelic train"

A PHILLIS rises, and the world no more
Denies the sacred right to mental pow'r;
While, Heav'n-inspired, she proves her Country's claim
To Freedom, and her own to deathless Fame.

—MATILDA, 1796

Hailed as a child prodigy, Phillis Wheatley, at the age of eighteen, became the first woman in 120 years to publish a freestanding volume of poetry in the New World—in fact, since Anne Bradstreet. Wheatley's story begins July 11, 1761. Aboard a schooner named *Phillis*, Wheatley was brought from West Africa to Boston. Apparently six or seven years of age, "from the circumstance of shedding her front teeth," Wheatley was at a wharf on Beach Street, near the home of a seasoned agent for slave ship captains, John Avery. The cargo was cleaned, greased, and made presentable for sale. Avery advertised in the *Boston Evening Post* and the *Boston Gazette and Country Journal* on July 29:

> To Be Sold
> A Parcel of likely Negroes, imported from Africa, cheap for cash, or short credit; Enquire of John Avery, at his House next Door to the White-Horse, or at a Store adjoining to said Avery's DistillHouse, at the South End, near the South Market; Also, if any Persons have any Negro Men, strong and hearty, tho' not of the best moral character, which are proper Subjects for Transportation, any have an Exchange for small Negroes. (Robinson 5)

A Wheatley descendant described the small female child among the "Parcel of likely Negroes":

> Aunt Wheatley was in want of a domestic. She went aboard to purchase. In looking through the ship's company of living freight, her attention was drawn to that of a slender, frail, female child, which at once enlisted her sympathies. Owing to the frailty of the child, she procured her for a trifle, as the captain had fears of her dropping off his hand, without emolument, by death. (Robinson 5)

Mistress Susanna Wheatley acquired the young black girl as a personal domestic for a mere 10 sterlings—a bargain, since the standard price for a prime male slave was 35 sterlings. As Wheatley's first biographer, another descendant of the Wheatley family, described:

> [The Mistress] visited the slave market, that she might make a personal selection from the group of unfortunates offered for sale; There she found several robust, healthy females, exhibited at the same time with Phillis, who was of a slender frame, and evidently suffering from change of climate. She was, however, the choice of the lady, who acknowledged herself influenced to this decision by the humble and modest demeanor and the interesting features of the little stranger. The poor, naked child, (for she had no other covering than a quantity of dirty carpet about her like a fillibeg) was taken home in the chaise of her mistress, and comfortably attired. (Robinson 6)

Named after the schooner that brought her to Boston, Phillis Wheatley arrived at the Wheatley home, located at the corner of King Street and Mekeral Lane (present-day State and Kilby Streets), becoming the newest addition to the staff of domestic slaves who cared for the their master, mistress, and two eighteen-year-old twins, Nathaniel and Mary.

Within a little more than a year, Phillis Wheatley was speaking and reading English proficiently. John Wheatley recounts in the preface to her book:

> Phillis was brought from *Africa* to *America,* in the Year 1761, between Seven and Eight Years of Age. Without any Assistance from School Education, and by only what she was taught in the Family, she, in sixteen Months Time from her Arrival, attained the English Language, to which she was an utter Stranger before, to such a Degree, as to read any, the most difficult Parts of the Sacred Writings, to the great Astonishment of all who heard her. (Robinson 149)

He claimed that Phillis's own "Curiosity" led her to learn. The Bible served as her first primer, and her exposure laid the religious foundation that is so apparent in her work.

Described as "obviously precocious" by Mary Wheatley, Phillis was tutored by both Susanna and Mary, gaining an extraordinary education for a young woman at that time, especially a slave. In 1765, just four years after Phillis Wheatley's purchase, Boston's population was 15,520, 1,000 of whom were blacks, 18 of whom were free. There were no black children among the 800 youth who attended the two grammar or Latin schools and the three vocational writing schools. Blacks in the American colonies were forcibly relegated into fixed inferior positions of menial servitude if free, or domestic service if owned. Although life for a New England colonial slave did not entail laboring in the fields of colonial plantations such as those existing in Virginia, Georgia, or the Carolinas, black New England slaves were just as exploited. Phillis Wheatley was a "curious" anomaly, her own counterculture to the Boston of her day.

By the age of eleven Wheatley had composed her first known piece of writing, a letter to a family friend, the minister Samson Occom. In 1776, Occom raised money with the minister Nathaniel Whitaker, in Scotland and England, to fund the education of Native Americans in New England. The school that Occom and Whitaker founded later became Dartmouth, a Methodist college, named after William Legge, Earl of Dartmouth, another one of Wheatley's correspondents and the subject of one of her poems. Wheatley's first published poem, "On Messrs. Hussey and Coffin," appeared on December 21, 1767, in the *Newport Mercury,* marking the start of her poetic "career." Wheatley's literary achievements quickly spread throughout Old and New England, along with her popularity, as she continued publishing in numerous newspapers and broadsides. Her increasing popularity led to the publication of her full, freestanding volume of poetry, *Poems on Various Subjects, Religious and Moral*, in 1773.

Much of Wheatley scholarship scrutinizes, at times harshly, her use of neoclassical conventions, her polite passivity regarding her racial experience, and issues of literary merit. Some scholars have disdain for her poetry, calling it mimicry of "white" culture, as she "submissively" performed for parlor audiences, fashioning herself and her subject matter to eventually gain access to readers through popularly distributed print media. Imamu Amiri Baraka criticizes Wheatley as an "imitator of Alexander Pope." In his evaluation of Wheatley's poem "On Being Brought from Africa to America," Baraka indicts her for "evincing gratitude from slavery" (139). His blatant attack on her poetry derives from his belief that Phillis was celebrating her slave masters. At one point Baraka compares Wheatley to Frankenstein's monster: "How wise, how omniscient be her creator" (139). African American literature produced in the eighteenth and nineteenth centuries was labeled "the Mockingbird School," since "these writers did not include anything 'specifically Negro'" (Foster 24).

I. TO BE A SLAVE IN PRINT: PREFATORY POLITICS

"On Being Brought from Africa" reads:

> 'Twas mercy brought me from my *Pagan* land,
> Taught my benighted soul to understanding
> That there's a God, that there's a *Saviour* too:
> Once I redemption neither sought nor knew.
> Some view our sable race with scornful eye,
> "Their colour is a diabolic die."
> Remember, *Christians, Negroes,* black as *Cain,*
> May be refin'd, and join th'angelic train. (Wheatley 53)

Even at age fifteen, when these lines were first penned, Wheatley seems to understand social prejudices and religious mythology. She considers herself fortunate to have found salvation, "refin'd" by education and the church, while dually reminding readers in the final couplet that it is their duty as Christians to cultivate the moral and intellectual nature of "Negroes" so that "they too may enjoy spiritual if not social equality" (Bell 184). Originally circulated among the Wheatleys and their friends, this poem and others created a local reputation for the young slave girl. J. Saunders Redding wrote in *To Make a Poet Black* (1939), "The Wheatleys had adopted her, but she had adopted their terrific New England conscience" (Bell 184). Subtly through her words, Wheatley assimilated herself into Boston society, using her unique status to move from the private to the public coterie.

Wheatley's poetry offers clues regarding her emergence into the marketplace as a black female slave writer. It is important to begin by examining the prefatory material that frames her work. The prefatory remarks outline the context that made Wheatley's transmission into the public coterie possible. Often quoted, Thomas Jefferson comments that "Among blacks is misery enough, God knows, but no poetry. . . . Religion indeed has produced a Phyllis Whately [*sic*]; but it could not produce a poet" (Jefferson 267). Though Jefferson dismisses Wheatley's talents, there is a piece of truth in his words. As unique as Wheatley appeared to her contemporary audiences, she was not the first female or the first black (free or slave) person to write. What was unique, however, was her social positioning within Boston, particularly within the Methodist church, which provided the necessary network for Wheatley to gain social agency.

To better understand the uniqueness of Wheatley's social position, it is useful to examine other slave writers of the time. Two of the most well-known slave writers preceding Wheatley were Lucy Terry Prince and Jupiter Hammon. Twenty years before Wheatley began publishing, sixteen-year-old

Lucy Terry wrote the often sung ballad "Bar's Fight," the "fullest contemporary account" captured on record of the Indian attack that occurred August 25, 1746, in Deerfield, Massachusetts (Sheldon 899). Critic Frances Foster describes "Bar's Fight" as:

> a straightforward, simply rhymed narrative commemorating an altercation between Indians and colonists in a frontier settlement. . . . This skirmish was not one of colonial America's most significant battles; however, because of this writer, its victims are memorialized while countless others are not. The poem is not one of colonial America's most elegant either; but it is appealing enough to have become a ballad sung by several generations of New Englanders and to be published in the *History of Western Massachusetts* over one hundred years after its creation. (23-24)

Created to memorialize a particular event of local importance, "Bar's Fight" is a good example of eighteenth-century occasional poetry, similar to that of Phillis Wheatley. The narrator avoids direct commentary or analysis, focusing instead on describing the climactic event. The construction of the poem makes it simple to comprehend and memorize.

Although Lucy Terry never gained the published prestige of Wheatley, George Sheldon offers Terry a prominent position in *The History of Deerfield.* He recounts that Terry was a visible participant in the black community (901). According to Sheldon, Terry was an established poet who held readings at her house, and he maintains that she composed at least two versions of "Bar's Fight." The historian John Hope Franklin writes that she had "a seemingly limitless store of tales about Africa and other faraway places that filled many an hour with excitement and pleasure" (66). None of her other poetry survives, and the specifics of her writings are now lost. The details of her emancipation are also unclear, but Sheldon does document that at the age of fourteen she was "admitted into the fellowship of the church" where she met her husband, Abijah Prince, a free black landholder from a neighboring town (55). Terry was known for her "wit and shrewdness" in arguing her side of a land ownership dispute before the Supreme Court. Presiding Justice Chase declared that she "made a better argument than he had heard from any lawyer at the Vermont bar" (Sheldon 950).

In another celebrated instance, she addressed the Williams College board of trustees with "an earnest and eloquent speech of three hours, quoting an abundance of law and Gospel, chapter and verse," in a futile attempt to change their rejection based on race of her son's application for admission (Sheldon 900). The historian Sidney Kaplan states that Lucy Terry became a model for other African American women, including her own daughter, Durexa, who enjoyed a reputation as a poet (211). Although Terry clearly claimed some form of public notoriety then, especially within an oral context, she never gained the agency that propelled Wheatley into a transatlantic icon.

Two other slave writers emerged onto the stage in 1760. Jupiter Hammon, a Long Island slave, published the eighty-eight-line broadside poem "An Evening Thought: Salvation by Christ with Penitential Cries." Hammon was the first black American to publish a poem in the colonies. The second to emerge was Briton Hammon "a Negro man, Servant to General Winslow of Marshfield, in New England," who published the fourteen-page pamphlet *A Narrative of the Uncommon Sufferings and Surprising Deliverance of Briton Hammon* (Foster 30). There is no other account of Briton Hammon in historical records. Jupiter Hammon, however, published another poem in 1778, this one praising Phillis Wheatley after she had become a well-established poet. In "AN ADDRESS to Miss PHILLIS WHEATLEY, Ethiopian Poetess, in Boston, who came from Africa at eight years of age, and soon became acquainted with the Gospel of Jesus Christ," Hammon's quatrains trace the spiritual journey of Wheatley as a "pious youth" from a "distant shore" to a Christian convert.

Jupiter Hammon's life exists in scraps of information found in his letters, poetry, and prose. Born a slave on October 17, 1711, he was owned by the Lloyds, a Long Island merchant family. Appearing intelligent and dutiful, Hammon was encouraged to read and write by his first master, Henry Lloyd; in one of his letters, Hammon mentions reading "the English divines, Burkitt and Beveridge," whose works were part of Lloyd's library (Bell 176). In 1733, Hammon purchased a Bible from his master for seven shillings and six pence. The notable biblical references that abound in his poetry, especially his Wheatley poem, exemplify how familiar Hammon was with the Bible. Unlike Lucy Terry and Wheatley, Hammon never gained his freedom. Upon the death of Henry Lloyd in 1763, three years after Hammon published his first broadside piece, Hammon was inherited by Joseph, one of the four sons. After Joseph's death during the Revolutionary War, the family retainer was passed to John Lloyd Jr. With the British occupation of Long Island, the patriotic Lloyd family moved to Hartford, Connecticut, taking Hammon with them (Bell 177).

It was in Hartford that Hammon published his poem on Wheatley, reestablishing himself as a published figure. Hammon died a slave around 1800, even though slavery was abolished in the state in 1784 (Bell 177). Although Hammon gained the prominent position of being the "first slave to publish within the colonies" and reestablished himself as a writer on the coattails of Wheatley's success, he never gained the positive attention that offered Wheatley the ability to participate in cultural exchange, giving her the agency to transform her position as slave. Jupiter Hammon may have produced more writing, but Wheatley managed to gain notoriety as a transatlantic "genius," thus becoming the first slave, male or female, to publish a book on both sides of the Atlantic.

Bernard Bell argues that the real "genius" of Wheatley's success as a writer, compared to other blacks, slaves or free, was not because of her actual literary abilities but because she "was more capable of coping with and giving poetic form to two planes of reality" (Bell 178). Wheatley maintained her subservient position as a slave while circulating in the social circles of her "white" readers. Bell notes that Jupiter Hammon's "unimaginative use of the meter, rhyme, diction, and stanza pattern of the Methodist hymnal combined with the negative image of Africa and conciliatory tone of these early poems reveal the poet's limitations and the costly socio-psychological price he paid for the mere semblance of cultural assimilation" (178). Bell's assessment of Hammon's inability to properly "assimilate" into culture, offers testimony to Wheatley's accomplishments. What "made" Wheatley, as Jefferson negatively suggests in his derogatory remarks on her writing, was her Methodist connections; "religion indeed produced" Wheatley. When examining Wheatley's success it is apparent that her position within colonial Boston, not just as a slave but as a "Wheatley" slave, gave her opportunities to network within the Wheatleys' religious political circles, allowing her to "assimilate" into culture and become not just a published writer but a kind of poet laureate in Old and New England.

Just as Anne Bradstreet used the prologue and prefatory material to introduce herself as an author by carefully controlling the reader's perceptions, Phillis Wheatley begins her preface similarly:

> The following Poems were written originally for the Amusement of the Author, as they were the products of her leisure Moments. She had no Intention ever to have published them; nor would they now have made their Appearance, but at the Importunity of many of her best, and most generous Friends; to whom she considers herself, as under the greatest Obligations. (Wheatley 45)

Indicative of eighteenth-century publishing, this traditional protest simultaneously controls the reader's perception of Phillis Wheatley, assuring the reader that she is not neglecting her role as a woman and a slave. The performative nature of the preface is further evident as Wheatley constructs her identity in the third person instead of the traditional first person. Referring to herself as "her" and "she," Wheatley creates a schism between the self who wrote the poems and the image of herself that the reader meets through third person introductions. By using the third person, Wheatley subordinates herself to her readers, who have the ability to claim the "I" pronoun as free citizens. Being a slave, Wheatley has no property rights, not even to herself, and she carefully constructs her apology to ensure that she does not claim equality with the reader.

The artificiality of her self-construction extends further in the preface. Wheatley explains to the reader that these poems were written as "amusements of the author," products of her "leisure moments." Trying to assure the reader that she is not neglecting her role as a slave or overstepping her boundaries, Wheatley makes it seem as if writing is a mere hobby she enjoyed between her chores. However, if she were treated as a slave, Wheatley would have had no "leisure moments." Further denying her intentions, Wheatley echoes Bradstreet's claim from almost 150 years earlier that she never intended to publish, yet "her best and most generous Friends" took it upon themselves to "make" her work public without her consent. Of course the same fallacy arises that was apparent with Bradstreet's claim. The poetry could not have been published without Wheatley's giving her friends access to the poems. Wheatley utilizes the rhetoric of "modesty and self-denial," wielding the same convention of the "reluctant and apologetic public speaker" that Bradstreet used to shape readers' expectations in her prefatory material.

The tone here shifts from an apologetic explanation to a tone of self-deprecation and self-consciousness, again indicative of earlier writers such as Bradstreet. Wheatley writes that "it is hoped that the Critic will not severely censure their Defects," and she describes her work as "worthless and trifling essusions" (Wheatley 46). A few lines later she pleads, "With all their Imperfections, the Poems are now humbly submitted to the Perusal of the Public" (46). Wheatley embraces the ideology that constrains her as a slave, that she is not capable of writing, and thus that there is no reason for readers to feel threatened by her ability to challenge their expectations. By humbling herself to the reader she appears to maintain a submissive position, when in fact she is subverting it by becoming a published writer.

Reinforcing the performative nature of Wheatley's prefatory remarks is "a Copy of a Letter sent by the Author's master to the Publisher" by John Wheatley, or so he claims (Wheatley 47). There is evidence that John Wheatley's claim to have composed his letter of attestation is false. In reality, Wheatley composed the letter herself. A one-paragraph version for her 1772 proposals is written in Wheatley's own handwriting. This later version she probably composed while sailing to London (Robinson 403). Wheatley's uncanny ability to step into her master's position, writing from his vantage point, allowed her to tinker with the reader's reality. If the reader believes that this letter was written by John Wheatley it indeed assures the reader that Wheatley is an anomaly, a young genius who demonstrates "a great Inclination to learn," making it clear that she has not been given any extra privileges as a slave. He writes:

Phillis was brought from *Africa* to *America,* in the Year 1761, between Seven and Eight Years of Age. Without any Assistance from School Education, and by only what she was taught in the Family, she, in sixteen Months Times from her Arrival, attained the English Language, to which she was an utter Stranger before, to such a Degree, as to read any, the most difficult Parts of the Sacred Writings, to the great Astonishment of all who heard her. (Wheatley 47)

Slaves who could read and write were rare. John Wheatley's statement becomes a testament to her "genius." In the next paragraph he states:

As to her Writing, her own Curiosity led her to it; and this she learnt in so short a Time, that in the Year 1765, she wrote a Letter to the Rev. Mr. Occom, the *Indian* Minister, while in England. (47)

This testament to Wheatley's "unexpected genius" serves an important purpose for Wheatley but also for the Wheatley family, whose abolitionist sentiments were well-known in Boston. Like Wheatley herself, they do not want to be perceived as overstepping their roles as her master. Worried about possible backlash against the family by readers for teaching their slave, John Wheatley claims that they had nothing much to do with it. Phillis learned "without any assistance," except what she learned by being around the family as a house slave. And, to further play on readers' sympathies, John Wheatley states that Phillis reads "the most difficult Parts of the Sacred Scriptures." As "good" Christians, whether abolitionist or not, it would be very difficult to condemn Phillis, since she is reading religious writings. By the last paragraph, the reader is given final assurance that Phillis Wheatley, although she "has a great Inclination to learn the Latin Tongue, and has made some Progress in it," she is still a slave, "bought by her Master . . . and with whom she now lives" (Wheatley 47).

Wheatley's and her master's prefatory claim that she wrote these poems herself is of course further supported by the attestation "signed by the above Gentlemen" (Wheatley 48). The witness list includes familiar names of well-known and even notorious men such as John Hancock, Lieutenant Governor Andrew Oliver, and even the governor himself, Thomas Hutchinson. It is important to note, however, that the first volumes of her book produced in London did not have the dedication, the preface, the biographical sketch, or the attestation, which are in most copies of the first edition (Robinson 404). Instead it was printed in newspaper ads, appearing in *Lloyd's Evening Post* and the *British Chronicle,* and in one newspaper the original statement is dated October 28, 1772 (Robinson 404). The newspaper ads served as the advertisement for readers to purchase additional copies of the later print run, which did include the prefatory material. The attestation by these respectable men offers legitimacy and in turn makes these otherwise seemingly demure occasional poems highly political. The oral examination performed by these eyewitness is important because:

If she had indeed written her poems, then this would demonstrate that Africans were human beings and should be liberated from slavery. If, on the other hand, she had not written, or could not write her poems, or if indeed she was like a parrot who speaks a few words plainly, then that would be another matter entirely. Essentially, she was auditioning for the humanity of the entire African people. (Gates 26-7)

Wheatley's writing, if truly written by her, provided the evidence needed to add momentum to the abolitionist movement. To properly convince the public, Gates explains the necessity for holding the assembly of Boston thinkers. Although private, one-on-one examinations of Wheatley's legitimacy were conducted, readers still questioned her abilities. One such private meeting was with the emissary to the Earl of Dartmouth, Thomas Woodbridge, who visited the Wheatley mansion, and wrote to the earl, stating:

While in Boston, I heard of a very Extraordinary female Slave, who made verses on our mutually dear deceased Friend [Whitefield]; I visited her mistress, and found by conversing with the African, that she was no Imposter; I asked if she could write on any Subject; she said Yes; we had just heard of your Lordships Appointment; I gave her your name, which she was well acquainted with. She immediately, wrote a rough Copy of the inclosed Address & Letter, with I promised to convey or deliver. I was astonished, and could hardly believe my own Eyes. I was present when she wrote, and can attest that it is her own production; she shewd me her Letter to Lady Huntington [sic], which, I dare say, Your Lordships has seen; I send you an Account signed by her master of her Importation, Education &.c They are all wrote in her own hand. (Gates 27-8)

Yet the reading public, especially in Boston, remained skeptical, making it necessary to publicly interrogate the young poet, otherwise no American publisher or reader would regard her writing with any seriousness. The public attestation was essential to the success of Wheatley's book and to the success of the abolitionist cause that Wheatley so well represented.

In addition, while proving that Wheatley is the volume's true author, the list of names also provides the pieces of unspoken history that reconstruct the highly political social network that Wheatley used to gain the public agency that granted her publication and her freedom, enabling her to rise above the prescribed roles that Lucy Terry and Jupiter Hammon were incapable of escaping.

Who were these gentlemen? All were respected men of position and influence and connected to the Wheatley family through social relations, business, or church. Robinson points out in his study of Wheatley that many of the signers were related by blood or marriage (270). Many attended or were in some way connected to Harvard College. Several of them, including Andrew Oliver, Thomas Hubbard, James Bowdoin, Samuel Cooper, Charles Chauncy, and John Moorhead, are subjects in Wheatley's poems. John Erving, Harrison Gray, and John Hancock were prominent Boston merchants who did business with John Wheatley, who was also a merchant. Joseph Green was also a merchant who knew the Wheatley family through business, and he also invited the young poetess to borrow books from his large library. Many of the signers were also connected by their affiliation with the Congregationalist church, a branch of the Methodist church in England and aligned with the abolitionist movement both in the colonies and England. Samuel Mather Byles was a Congregationalist minister. Samuel Mather Byles, son of Cotton Mather, was pastor of the Tenth Congregationalist Church. Ebenezer Pemberton was pastor of the Congregationalist New Brick Church in the North End. Andrew Eliot was pastor of the Congregationalist New North Church, and his antislavery views were well-known, as were those of Harrison Gray. The other signers all appear on church attendance rosters at the various local Congregationalist churches. In many ways, it is religion that connects these men to Wheatley, who was herself a baptized member of the Congregationalist church.

Indeed, religion ultimately secured the patronage Wheatley needed to publish her book. After publishing several poems, a proposal for book publication was submitted to Boston publishers in 1772. Her proposal was quickly dismissed for reasons that are unclear. Some critics attribute the lack of support to the political climate of Boston at the time. Publishers were focusing more on printing pre-Revolutionary propaganda pamphlets than books of poetry. The rising cost of manufacturing and purchasing goods also attributed to the lack of interest in publishing a full-length volume, since readers did not have extra money to spend on books. Broadsides were cheap in comparison. Other scholars, such as Henry Louis Gates, speculate that the climate of Boston was not conducive for a black writer, especially a slave writer, as evidenced by the need to have the attached attestation. In many ways, although Boston readers, specifically elite Bostonians, enjoyed Wheatley as an anomaly, they were not ready to support the notion that people of color could produce books. Whatever the circumstances, it became quickly apparent that support for publication was going to have to be found elsewhere.

While attending the Congregationalist church with her mistress, Susanna Wheatley, Phillis met the Reverend George Whitefield, a well-spoken, flaming evangelist. Whitefield preached a total of four times during the month of August 1770 before dying suddenly in Newburyport, Massachusetts. His death prompted Wheatley to write her famous elegy "On the Death of Rev. George Whitefield." Publication of this poem in various papers throughout the colonies and in England gained Wheatley fame on both sides of the Atlantic. The promotion of the poem eventually reached important figures in England, including William Legge, the Earl of Dartmouth, "His Majesty's Principal Secretary of State for North America," John Thornton, a wealthy millionaire and Christian philanthropist, and Selina Hastings, the Countess of Huntingdon. Whitefield served as the countess's personal chaplain. Deeply moved by Wheatley's eulogy and connected to the Wheatley family indirectly through religious circles, the countess offered to serve as Phillis's English patron, networking her into elite circles of funding and support in England.

In fact, it was the countess who secured the services of the English publisher Archibald Bell, a London bookseller who focused on religious works. The 1773 proposal was carried to Bell by acting representative of the Wheatley family, Captain Robert Calef of the Wheatley-owned *London*, which made regular trips between Boston and London. Calef also transferred the documentation of attestation to Bell, along with Phillis's desire to have the book dedicated to the countess. Ultimately it was Bell who approached the countess about Wheatley's desire to honor her through the dedication. A letter written by Susanna Wheatley to Samson Occom, dated March 29, 1773, details the exchange between the countess and Bell. An excerpt from the letter, now held among the Samson Occom papers at the Connecticut Historical Society, reads:

> The following is an Extract from Capt Calef's Letter dates Jan 7th. "Mr. Bell (the printer) acquaints me that about 5 weeks ago he waited upon the Countess of Huntingdon with the Poems, who was greatly pleas'd with them; and often would break in on him and Say, 'is not this, or that, very fine? do read another,' and then expressed herself, She found her heart to knit with her and Question'd him much, whether She was Real without a deception? He then Convinc'd her by bringing my Name [Calef] in question. She is expected in Town in a Short time when we are both to wait upon her. I had like to forget to mention to you She is fond of having the Book Dedicated to her; but one this She desir'd which She Said She hardly tho't would be denied her, that was to have Phillis' picture in the frontpiece. So that if you would get it done it can be Engrav'd here, I do imagine it can be Easily done, and think would contribute greatly to the Sale of the Book." (Mason 7)

The countess obviously is thrilled by the notion of being associated with a "genius" such as Wheatley.

Dedicating the book to the countess was a shrewd move because the countess's endorsement elevated the status of the book and of Wheatley as a writer and made it easier for Wheatley to "sell" herself to readers. Being publicly associated with the countess, a figure of great prominence, gave Wheatley authority with readers. To the reader she appeared as more than just a slave or a prodigy; she was part of the countess's inner circle. This public association enabled Wheatley to network after her arrival in London. During her brief month-and-a-half visit she was invited to participate in social and literary activities as if she were a countess herself. As Robinson describes Phillis's reception, "She was an acknowledged celebrity among fellow celebrities and English peers" (34). She wrote on October 18, 1773, to Col. David Wooster of New Haven, a friend and supporter of her literary activity, shortly after her arrival back in Boston:

> I was receiv'd in England with such kindness Complaisance, and many marks of esteem and reall Friendship as astonishes me on the reflection, for I was no more the 6 weeks there—Was introduced to Lord Dartmouth and near half an hour's conversation with his Lordship, with whom was Adlerman Kirkman,—Then to Lord Lincoln, who visited me at my own Lodgings with the Famous Dr. Solander, who accompany'd Mr. Banks in his late expedition round the World. Then to Lady Cavendish, and Lady Carteret Webb,—Mrs. Palmer a Poetress, an accomplish'd Lady.—Dr. Thos Gibbons, Phetoric Professor, To Israle Mauduit Esq. who attended me to the Tower & show'd the Lions, Panthers, Tigers & The Horse Armoury, small Armoury, the Crowns, Sceptres, Diadems, the Font forget christening the Royal Family, Saw Westminister Abbey, British Museum, Coxes Museum, Saddler's wells, Greenwich Hospital, Park and Chapel, the royal Observatory at Greenwich, &c&c too many things & places to trouble with in a Letter.—The Earl of Dartmouth made me a Compliment of 5 Guineas, and desir'd me to get the whole of Mr. Pope's Works, as their he could recommend to my perusal, this I did, also got Hudibrass, Don Quixote & Gay's Fables—was presented with a Folio Edition of Milton's Paradise Lost, printed on Silver Type. (Wheatley, Penguin Ed., 147)

Her connections extended beyond those mentioned in the letter. She visited John Thorton and his family of four children; Baron George Lyttelton, distinguished English statesman and man of letters; the Reverend Dr. James Thomas; and Captain Calef's family in nearby Homerton (Robinson 35). All of these individuals, with the exception of Captain Calef, were in some way connected to the countess and facilitated Phillis's invitation to be presented to the king and queen of England. Wheatley never met the countess in person, but her seeming affiliation with her allowed Phillis the social mobility needed to elevate her, claim her position of authority, and participate in the process of producing her book. Through her religious and social relationships, Wheatley became the active creator and owner of her work.

Not only was Wheatley received more "equally" as a result of her association with the countess, but the dedication allowed readers to enjoy the same sense of social mobility, or at least feel more "equal." By purchasing and reading the same texts that were available to the elite class, middle-class readers became empowered participants in cultural exchange. Dedicating the book to such an influential, privileged individual, helped sell the book. Readers would buy it for the sheer imaginative power of being associated with the countess through a type of "virtual" proximity. It is no accident that the promotional material included her poem "Farewel to America" in several newspapers throughout New England, New York, and Pennsylvania. Newspapers printed notices of Phillis's pending departure for London, followed by advertisement of her upcoming book. After Wheatley's departure, upon the request of Susanna Wheatley in a letter dated May 10, 1773, the *London Chronicle* published the poem. Robinson remarks that the timely reprint in the *Boston Post Boy* on March 1, 1773, and in the *Essex Gazette* on March 16-23 of Wheatley's poem "Recollection" was complete with the original accompanying letter by "L" and the note by Phillis to the dedicatee, "Madam," all of which had been first printed in the *London Magazine* in March 1772 (32). The April issues of the *News Letter* and the *Post Boy and the Advertiser* printed advertisements for "Proposals / for printing in London by Subscription, / A volume of Poems, / Dedicated by Permission to the Right Hon. the / Countess of Huntingdon / Written by Phillis, / A negro Servant of Mr. Wheatley, of Boston / in New England" (Robinson 32). Even after her departure from London, Phillis's association with the countess was evident to the public. On May 6 the *Boston Post Boy and Advertiser* reported, "The Ship London, Capt Calef sails on Saturday / for London, in whom goes passengers Mr. Nathaniel Wheatley / Merchant, also Phillis, Servant to Mr. Wheatley the extraordinary Negro poet, at the Invi- / tation of the Countess of Huntingdon" (Robinson 34). A second print with a "correction" occurred in the same paper on May 13. Similar promotions occurred in England. Bell submitted to several newspapers a lengthy notice, which included a bold statement about the dedication. In *Lloyd's Evening Post and British Chronicle* on September 10-13 and 13-15, and in the *Public Advertiser* the notice read, "Dedicated, by Permission, to the Right Hon. / the Countess of Huntingdon. / *This Day is Published,* /Price 2s. Sewed, or 2s. 6D neatly bound, adorned with / an elegant Likeness of the Author" (Robinson 38). A variant of this notice appeared in the *London Chronicle* on September 9-11, 11-14, and in the *London Morning Post and Daily Advertiser* on September 13 (38). With hopes of promoting sales, readers on both sides of the ocean were made aware that Wheatley was part of the countess's inner circle.

The prefatory material certainly helped promote Wheatley and her book. Ironically, all of Wheatley's social and religious connections, including the eighteen witnesses who signed the attestation, were slaveholders. Henry Louis Gates Jr. documents that:

Thomas Hubbard had actually been a dealer in slaves. Even the venerable James Bowdoin bought and sold slaves in the 1760s, while we know from Joseph Green's will that he left one hundred pounds to his slave "Plato."

Another, the Reverend Charles Chauncy, in 1743, had attacked the Great Awakening because it allowed "women and girls; yea Negroes—to do the business of preachers" (8).

George Whitefield had owned at least fifty slaves. He purchased them with money he received from a special grant in 1764 for the purpose of clearing 2,000 acres of land located twelve miles outside of Savannah, Georgia, for the building of Bethesda, his orphanage house (Robinson 108). In a letter to the *Massachusetts Gazette and Boston Weekly News Letter* that appeared on February 8, 1770, an "alarmed Bostonian professed great surprise and dismay and disgust" upon hearing of Whitefield's hypocritical action of holding slaves. The reader was:

> greatly surprised and grieved, not long since, to find *Mr. Whitefield's* Memorial to the Governor and Council of *Georgia*; that his plan is to buy Number of Negroe Slaves, whose Labors are to support the President, Professors, and Tutors or his College, as well as Overseers. (Gates 109)

Whitefield's actions helped repeal the antislavery provision that had been a part of the original Georgia charter (Gates 109). Even the countess was a slaveholder. A copy of Whitefield's will, printed in the *Boston News Letter* on April 19, 1771, stated that the "buildings, lands, negroes, furniture" of Bethesda orphanage be bequeathed "to that elect lady, that mother of Israel, that mirror of true and undefiled religion, Right Honorable Selina, Countess Dowager of Huntingdon" (Robinson 109). Soon after learning of her inheritance, the countess sent a group of her own missionaries from London to Savannah to administer the estate. She ordered that profits from the first sales of the trust, amounting to a total of 26.05.65 pounds, were to be used to buy a female slave. The countess wrote, "I must request that a woman slave be purchased with it, and that she might be called Selina, after me" (Robinson 109). The American Quaker abolitionist Anthony Benezet wrote the countess, pointing out the hypocrisy of her slave buying in the colonies (109).

One would expect that individuals publicly supporting Wheatley in the prefatory material would be staunch abolitionists who held steadfast to their principles by not owning slaves. Although Wheatley's supporters were abolitionist sympathizers, they were not ready to apply principle to personal actions. Even Wheatley's owners did not grant manumission until the reading public demanded it. This dichotomy was not uncommon. Many of the Founding Fathers, including John Hancock, were supporters of abolitionist ideology, but because they wanted to ensure the ratification of the Declaration of Independence, all references to slavery were deleted. Colonists were not ready to make antislavery ideology a part of mass culture. Too many of them benefited economically from slave labor. Ironic and hypocritical as it may seem, this appears to have worked in Wheatley's favor. Had the prefatory material only included individuals who were extreme abolitionists, her book might not have been so widely accepted; it would have been too radical. Her book appeared nonthreatening to readers, since the politics are not blatant. More important, Wheatley herself appears nonthreatening to readers since she appears to stay within her prescribed role. Ultimately the focus was on the Wheatley's surprising genius. By acting as though she has joined "th'angelic train," she gained the agency needed to promote and sell her book. Phillis Wheatley's *Poems on Various Subjects, Religious and Moral* was published in early September and received a great deal of attention from the public in the London press. The book was sold in at least six locations in London and was popular throughout England and Scotland as well (Mason 8). The young slave girl became an overnight literary success.

II. THE POWER OF PASSIVITY: PHILLIS'S POETICS

If Phillis's prefatory gestures appear passive to contemporary readers, then the poetry that follows appears even more passive with its apparent lack of condemnation of slavery. Wheatley's poetics have received harsh criticism from readers who interpret her as a cultural ventriloquist, mimicking the behaviors and values of the society that controlled her like a parlor parrot. In many ways the charges levied against Wheatley are not unwarranted. In thirty-eight poems published in the 1773 edition, Wheatley's racialized experience appears obliquely, scattered throughout the various occasional poems as passing references to her native origins. While briefly referring to her "native land" provides a sense of outsider status, there are no direct statements regarding her enslavement except her allusion to her enslavement in her address to the Earl of Dartmouth. As Kristin Wilcox criticizes, "Words like 'iron chain' and 'enslave' . . . may have pointed attentive readers to Wheatley's servitude, but nowhere in her verse does she speak directly as a slave" (24).

It is easy as a contemporary reader to quickly dismiss Wheatley's poems and see her as a "sell out," but to dismiss her is to miss the subtlety of her work. Such cursory readings overlook the way in which Wheatley coyly "fashions" herself to gain agency with her audience. Wheatley chose not to employ eighteenth-century poetic techniques, such as searing satire and irony like that of Alexander Pope or Jonathan Swift, or the descriptive language that accompanied Puritan occasional poetry, like that of Sarah Knight. To use such conventions would have severely compromised her success with readers because she would have seemed too bold, overstepping her position as both a woman and slave. The muting of Wheatley's opinions "was a necessary consequence of her changed relationship to the reading public"; any "political subjectivity was denied her as a slave, an African, and a woman" (Wilcox 19). Thus, Wheatley "fashioned" herself in such a way as not to offend readers, since her publication heralded the "unprecedented participation of a black slave in the white and propertied sphere of print" (Wilcox 19). The liability of direct self-expression would have kept her from expression altogether; she had to embrace a more "passive" persona.

Wheatley was adept at "fashioning" herself, as evidenced by changes in the London edition compared to the Boston proposal. Wheatley understood that her book required a different configuration if she wanted to "sell" it to an audience outside "the sphere of common experience that connected Wheatley to Boston readers" (Wilcox 16). As Wilcox remarks:

> More significantly, London publication brought with it certain belletristic expectations that affected both what Wheatley printed there and how her literary authority would be construed. These expectations increased Wheatley's literary stature, but they also silenced her in ways that went beyond the simple censorship of mistress and marketplace. (17)

After significantly editing her original proposal, the collection of poems that appeared in England retained only fifteen poems of the original thirty-eight, and the titles of the remaining fifteen were revised to better suit London readers. Julian Mason comments on Wheatley's decision to rework the Boston proposal:

> Some of the poems listed in the Proposals were too American, too politically oriented in sensitive times, for England and the Wheatleys' friends there, so they were omitted. Others were changed some in light of the same concerns but were retained. Others were added. Some were simply made more generic for an audience for whom many of the local names would mean nothing. . . . The total number of poems increased by approximately one-fourth, and the book as a whole took on an even more religious cast, one not unsuited to the woman to whom it now was dedicated and her friends. (187)

In tracing American Revolutionary themes in Wheatley's verse Grimstead comments, "Two political poems remained in Wheatley's collection when the decision was made to publish in London and not Boston. Five were dropped on subjects such as America, the arrival of British troops, and the Boston Massacre," which occurred just a few blocks from the Wheatley residence

(339). In a footnote, he adds that seven poems "on personal or religious themes" were also omitted.

What was retained in the London volume was the focus on specific individuals and events. Wilcox proposes that the omission of five topical poems and the replacement of some of the proper names with generic signifiers was perhaps a move on Wheatley's part to make the poems seem less provincial (17). The London edition included eight new topical poems, for a total of eighteen occasional poems compared to fourteen originally proposed for the Boston edition. The two lyric poems named in the Boston proposal were joined by six more. Wheatley recognized the need to "refashion" the upcoming volume, focusing on broader allusions to "Freedom" and "grievances unredress'd," as Wheatley writes in "To the Right Honourable William, Earl of Dartmouth," than on the particulars of the patriot cause. Although she substantially revised which poems were included in the London edition, the typically neoclassical occasional poems still expressed Wheatley's political and religious views, but her opinions are from an avowedly passive position. As Wilcox argues, the subordination of her self-expression made "the collection more metropolitan, less involved with provincial particularity, even in the context of Wheatley's articulated American patriotism," a maneuver that allowed her the space to establish a stance of literary authority (21).

Wheatley's "self-fashioning" extends beyond the editorial changes in the London volume. On the surface, Wheatley's selective self-representation in the content of her poetry seems to reflect a constrained authorial voice, a passive observer who cameos various famous individuals in a typical neoclassical elegiac style. In our contemporary culture, being an agent of another rather than a self-determining individual is an undesirable, anxiety-ridden, and disempowered position. However, as Stephen Greenblatt describes in *Renaissance Self-Fashioning*, this is not the case in early modern texts. Expecting to find that Renaissance "middle-class and aristocratic males" felt that "they possessed . . . shaping power over their lives," he discovered instead that in these texts "the human subject itself began to seem remarkably unfree" (256). After "exploring the ways in which major English writers of the sixteenth century created their own performances," Greenblatt concludes that "fashioning oneself and being fashioned by cultural institutions—family, religion, state—were inseparably intertwined. . . . If there remained traces of free choice, the choice was among possibilities whose range was strictly delineated by the social and ideological system in force" (256). Recent academic discourse reflects the notion that the loss of self-possession brings a corresponding sense of anxiety and alienation. Therefore to be "fashioned" or "self-fashioned" is a seemingly negative and passive authorial gesture.

Though Greenblatt's insights pertain to the Renaissance, his observations are germane to the seventeenth and eighteenth centuries. In a similar study, Leo Damrosch surveys Christian writing from Augustine to Fielding, noting that "the surrender of free will" provides "relief from desperate anxiety" (27). Scott Gordon explains in his study of seventeenth- and eighteenth-century discourse, "These writers desire not to be a self-determining agent but rather to be an agent of another: abandoning the assertion of free will, they desire to believe their actions have been prompted by another force" (21). Using what he calls the "passivity trope," Gordon argues that:

> for many writers "being fashioned," being "acted by another," offers reassurance rather than anxiety, relief rather than despair: our obsession with self-reliance, self-sufficiency, and independence privileges a series of values these writers actively reject. The empowerment of individual agents by early modern and Enlightenment discourse strengthens a competing discourse that endorses a form of subjectivity subordinating individuals as actors in a drama written by another.
>
> Confronted with the naturalization of the dissociated, self-interested individual, many seventeenth- and eighteenth-century texts recoil—and to deny that image of humankind they use the passivity trope to insist, to imagine, that *dis*interested behavior is possible. (Gordon 6)

Emerging from seventeenth-century Quaker and eighteenth-century Methodist insistence on refusing the sharp distinction between the elect and the few, along with the theology of universal availability of grace, disenfranchised groups had the possibility of free will, which had previously been denied them as passive recipients of God's. Gordon applies this religious discourse to recover a counter-tradition in eighteenth-century literature that imagines selves as more passively prompted than actively choosing, stating that writers:

> consistently construe[d] behaviors as passive (or natural) to deny that individuals calculate their interest. This construction locates the agency for such behaviors outside the individual to eliminate any space in which individuals could calculate their interest or even consider their audience.
>
> They try to "guarantee" that "outward behavior . . . is not the product of Pharisaic motivation," that is by imagining behaviors not in the individual will but elsewhere—sometimes in another individual, usually in external nature or God—and thus depict the agent as more passively prompted than actively choosing, more "acted by another" than acting freely. This discourse of passivity, what I call in this study "the passivity trope"—deployed by religious discourse, acting theory, moral philosophy, and the emergent novel—constructs a self whose disinterestedness is guaranteed by forces outside conscious control. (4-5)

Gordon makes it clear that this does not mean "unconscious" forces in the psychoanalytic sense but "external forces that work through the body and bypass the mind. These eighteenth-century discourses . . . imagine disinterested or non-rhetorical behavior only by constructing it as passive" (5).

By deploying a discourse of passivity, many writers represented the "self" as more formed than forming. They become actors on the stage, performing the lines delineated by their "natural" position. By acting within their prescribed roles, writers gained agency by appearing to passively perform as expected by society. Ironically, by controlling their image, passivity is transformed into a privilege rather than a curse, as the use of passivity submissively subverts readers' expectations. By *appearing* to conform, these eighteenth-century writers cause reform.

To access the marketplace Wheatley employed this eighteenth-century construction of identity originating from the legacy of Protestant. "Fashioning" herself to appear as a passive agent "acted upon" by her position as a young, black, slave, female writer, she keeps herself from becoming suspect to her readers, who would have condemned any direct attack she might have made directly on slavery. Wheatley's opinions about her own position seem nonexistent as she instead focuses on people, places, general politics, and religion. Wheatley was capable of biting irony and searing satire, which marked most social criticism of her time; suppression was a conscious choice on her part. In one of her most circulated publications for both royalist and patriot readers, published in 1774, Wheatley delivers one of her most scathing criticisms of her position as a slave. As she writes Samson Occom, she chastises the owners of slaves—both royalists and patriots alike. In piercing tones she explicitly attacks the hypocrisy of the people whom she called "modern Egyptians," who ironically cry for freedom yet end each day with tea served by their own house slaves. Wheatley writes, "How well the Cry for Liberty, and the reverse Disposition for the exercise of oppressive Power over others agree,—I humbly think it does not require the Penetration of a Philosopher to determine" (Mason 204-5). Wheatley knew how to be direct and voiced her position with disdain, yet in her poetry she chose to approach her audience much more subtly.

Although she is direct, the letter provides evidence of how Wheatley was able to maintain popular acceptance on both sides of the pre-Revolutionary struggle. The letter was published by Boston's most radical patriot leaders in the *Massachusetts Spy*. It was also published by Joseph Greenleaf, editor of the *Royal American Magazine*. By using the phrase "modern Egyptians" but never directly stating to whom she was referring, readers on both sides of the struggle assumed that she was talking about their adversary. Patriots interpreted "tyrant" and "modern Egyptians" as royalists, and royalists, such as the British pamphleteer Samuel Seabury, could turn the patriot metaphor of "slavery" back on the patriots and on the threatening idea of a republican government (Willard 237).

Wheatley's poetry takes the use of arbitrariness one step further, as she constructs a seemingly more passive authorial voice with the hope, as she writes in her letter to Occom, of "[convincing] them of the strange Absurdity of their Conduct whose Words and Actions are so diametrically opposite" (Mason 204). In her epistle to George III, Wheatley's use of pre-Revolutionary politics obscures her political position. The poem's tone is one of praise, a celebration of freedom that paradoxically the poet herself cannot enjoy. Originally written in 1768, it was titled "To the King's Most Excellent Majesty, On His Repeal of the Stamp Act." The title was altered for English audiences in the 1773 publication, reducing the reference to the Stamp Act to a mere footnote. Wheatley's African identity or position as a slave is not mentioned. Wheatley addresses the king as a passive observer, beginning with:

> Your subjects hope, dread Sire—
> The crown upon your brows may flourish long,
> O may your sceptre num'rous nations sway,
> And all with love and readiness obey! (Wheatley 53)

Wheatley circumvents her own identity by immediately using the plural "subjects," maintaining anonymity by omitting the use of the singular "I." She makes her cry of freedom as a "subject," not as a slave. Wheatley continues:

> But how shall we the *British* king reward!
> Rule thou in peace, our father, our lord!
> Midst the remembrance of thy favours past,
> The meanest peasants most admire the last.
> May *George*, belov'd by all the nations round,
> Live with heav'ns choicest constant blessings crown'd!
> Great God, direct, and guard him from on high,
> And from his head let ev'ry evil fly!
> And may each clime with equal gladness see
> A monarch's smile can set his subjects free! (Wheatley 53)

Downplaying the events of the Stamp Act, the poem becomes appealing to royalist readers. Wheatley quickly gains favor with her London audience as she praises the king for his "favours." Utilizing the conventions of occasional poetry, Wheatley catalogs a list of blessings for the king, who is portrayed as having godly power to emancipate. The extensive use of the apostrophe makes imperative her seeming respect for the king she is praising.

For patriot readers in Boston, the poem can be read in a completely different light. The plural "subjects" becomes arbitrary, making it unclear whom

Wheatley is including. As colonists they are also "subjects" of the king. The lines of praise, however, have a subtle sarcasm, especially when Wheatley addresses God, prayerfully asking God to "direct" the King and "let ev'ry evil fly" from his head. While sounding like a blessing to royalists, for a patriot reader, the tone elicits a dry, sarcastic commentary on how the king has poorly conducted himself, since he is obviously in need of God's guidance. Her lines make the king look less godly in his power, since he is in need of prayers. Thus by obscuring her own identity, Wheatley is able to maintain a rapport with readers, since her presence is completely diffused.

Or is it? Between the said and the unsaid, through the theme of mutual gratification, where "A monarch's smile can set his subjects free," Wheatley's poetry suddenly does not seem like simple parlor games. The content of the poem, focused on the Stamp Act repeal, becomes an address to all readers who act like "monarchs." Using pre-Revolutionary politics as metaphor, Wheatley secretly shakes her finger at the hypocritical behavior of all her readers. Superimposing "reward" and "favours" with "free," Wheatley "recalls the central proposition of the 'freedom' arguments which ignored the community of African American slaves" (Willard 241). The implications of the poem, though understated, are powerful, since Wheatley is a slave.

Wheatley's most anthologized poem, "On Being Brought from Africa to America," also listed in her 1772 proposal and originally dated 1768, portrays her as conforming to society's religious expectations. She seems to passively accept the salvation that joining "the angelic train" offers, and the poem's style is indicative of a common religious testimonial. To readers on both sides of the Atlantic, Wheatley fulfills their expectations regarding black slaves—that they are heathens in need of redemption, as she calls her homeland "pagan." She seems to condemn her own self, as she describes how she did not know about religion, or that "there's a God," and "there's a Saviour too." Wheatley's use of quotation marks around the phrase "Their colour is a diabolic die" seems to directly express the sentiments of her readers, as Wheatley passively performs the lines like an actor on a stage, repeating the scripted words of a director. The final couplet concludes the poem with submission to Protestant ethics, as Wheatley testifies that in order to be "refin'd" and saved, the reader must join the "angelic train."

Once again, on the surface, Wheatley appears to be a cultural ventriloquist, mimicking the religious convictions of the institution that makes slaves of individuals like herself while preaching salvation and redemption. However, once again, with dry sarcasm, Wheatley is not actually testifying but criticizing. If read with the same tone of biting irony and sarcasm as her address to King George, Wheatley's poem sends a very different message to the reader. Although she seems to condemn her own birthplace, calling it "pagan," where she does not know "religion," she is actually saying that there was no need to know of it, because there she was free. Since she was not a slave, she did not need to know or seek "redemption." It was only once she stepped on colonial soil that she was "taught . . . to understand." The repetition in the third line provides the answer regarding what Wheatley actually learned. Once again, the arbitrariness of the nouns "God" and "Saviour" allow Wheatley to point her finger at her readers, "modern Egyptians" who owned slaves. Wheatley's subtle understatement makes it clear that she understands who is really in control of her freedom. The last couplet perhaps holds the most irony; on the surface, Wheatley seems to uphold Protestant theology, but she actually exposes her readers' hypocritical actions because she is reminding "Christians" in very plain terms that even a black slave girl can "join" them, and that perhaps they are the ones in need of being "refin'd."

Wheatley's celebratory poems to individuals act as vehicles for her own agenda as she utilizes the epistles to attack the moral underpinnings of the belief in the inferior African. Like the speaker in "On Being Brought from Africa to America," the speaker in Wheatley's most famous epistle, "On the Death of the Rev. Mr. George Whitefield," preaches a doctrine of pervasive and divine impartiality. In this poem Wheatley uses voice to mask her argument. Printed often in 1770 with Wheatley's framing letter addressed directly to the countess of Huntingdon, the elegy was perhaps the most widely circulated of the poet's newspaper poems. Most copies of the poem circulated as broadsides, but one of the earliest versions was printed as an eight-page pamphlet, "Printed and Sold by Ezekiel Russell, in Queen-street, And John Boyles, in Marlboro'-street" in Boston (Mason 55).

Whitefield had an enormous following in the American colonies, as well as in Britain. Mass audiences yielded to the captivating power of Whitefield's evangelism, and Wheatley's elegies "balanced eulogy with hyperbole in a style that became popular for many of her contemporaries" (Willard 244). The poem begins with Wheatley's mourning Whitefield's death and an apostrophe celebrating his eloquence:

> HAIL, happy saint, on thine immortal throne,
> Possest of glory, life, and bliss unknown;
> We hear no more the music of thy tongue,
> Thy wonted auditories cease to throng.
> Thy sermons in unequall'd accents flow'd,
> And ev'ry bosom with devotion glow'd;
> Thou didst in strains of eloquence refin'd
> Inflame the heart, and captivate the mind.
> Unhappy we the setting sun deplore,
> So glorious once, but ah! It shines no more. (Wheatley 55-6)

Wheatley faithfully adheres to the eighteenth-century pattern as she turns elegy into epistle by speaking directly to the dead. In these first lines, Whitefield becomes the saintly evangelist, endowed with an extraordinary power of persuasion over his "wonted audiences." The fire imagery conjures up Whitefield's elegant oratory. Anyone who has attended a religious revival immediately connects with the imagery of mental burning, as one is captivated by the awe of such spiritual persuasion. Even the most level-headed of Christians, men like Benjamin Franklin, succumbed to the appeal of Whitefield's brilliant sermons, which convinced wide audiences of the urgent need to reject sin, promising them saintly ends under his evangelical wing (Willard 244).

The imagery shifts from fire to flight as Whitefield becomes a mythical bird, whose "incessant cries" move audiences to "excel" and "in their conduct shine."

> Behold the prophet in his tow'ring flight!
> He leaves the earth for heav'n's unmeasur'd height,
> And worlds unknown receive him from our sight.
> There *Whitefield* wings with rapid course his way,
> And sails to Zion through vast seas of day. (Wheatley 56)

Whitefield's greatness is further exaggerated by Wheatley's depiction of him flying to "unmeasur'd heights." As Whitefield soars, Wheatley tells the reader that it was his desire to see his audiences reach the same heights:

> He pray'd that grace in ev'ry heart might dwell,
> He long'd to see *America* excel;
> He charg'd its youth that ev'ry grace divine
> Should with full luster in their conduct shine;
> That Saviour, which is sould did first receive,
> The greatest gift that ev'n a God can give,
> He freely offer'd to the num'rous throng,
> That on his lips with list'ning pleasure hung. (Wheatley 56).

By the final couplet, the focus of the poem shifts. Wheatley begins summarizing Whitefield's ministry, and she notes with a bit of irony that he "freely" offered his eloquent words, although it was assumed that if one attended any of his sermons, an offering was expected.

By the next stanza, Wheatley places quotes around the phrases, implying that she is quoting the great minister himself:

> "Take him, ye wretched, for your only good,
> "Take him ye starving sinners, for your food;
> "Ye thirsty, come to this life-giving stream,

"Ye preachers, take him for your joyful theme;
"Take him my heart *Americans*, he said,
"Be your complaints on his kind bosom laid;
"Take him, ye *Africans*, he longs for you,
"*Impartial Saviour* is his title due:
"Wash'd in the fountain of redeeming blood,
"You shall be sons, and kings, and priests of God." (Wheatley 56)

The voice in the poems shifts from Wheatley to Whitefield as he takes the stage, preaching divine impartiality. By acting as if she is quoting Whitefield, Wheatley masks her presence in the poem. It is most ironic that Wheatley uses Whitefield as her vehicle to reach readers, since Whitefield himself owned slaves. Whitefield's words, though religious on the surface, become highly political, as he calls for unifying equality in the Christian family, which includes the *"Africans."* The ritual of baptism, the "fountain of redeeming blood," places *"Africans"* on an equal footing in the afterlife, since they, too, will be "sons, and kings, and priests of God," alongside *"Americans."* With the exception of writers like Anthony Benezet, John Woolman, and John Wesley, such earthly equality was rarely called for in Wheatley's time (Willard 245). By using Whitefield's eloquent, Wheatley is able to show the discrepancies of her own position as a slave as she argues that she, along with her Christian readers, are equal in the eyes of God.

Because "sons, and kings, and priests" are earthly, not heavenly, designations, these categories had the potential to create discord even among the most liberal of readers. Knowing this, Wheatley quickly inserts a second apostrophe as if to divert her readers' attention before they can accuse her of overstepping her boundaries as a slave.

Great *Countess*, we *Americans* revere
Thy name, and mingle in thy grief sincere;
New England deeply feels, the *Orphans* mourn,
Their more than father will no more return.

The voice shifts once again to Wheatley as she tells the countess how much Whitefield will be missed. Wheatley further unifies herself with her readers by using the pronoun "we." Together both *"Africans"* and *"Americans"* are once again joined, not only in heaven by God's divine impartiality but on earth as well through the act of grief.

In the last line the reference to "father" becomes oblique and continues into the next stanza:

But, though arrested by the hand of death,
Whitefield no more exerts his lab'ring breath,

> Yet let us view him in th' eternal skies,
> Let ev'ry heart to this bright vision rise;
> While the tomb safe retains it sacred trust,
> Till life divine re-animates his dust.

It is unclear whether Wheatley is referring to Whitefield as the "father" or to "God." The pronoun references blur, as Wheatley appeals to the reader, urging that "ev'ry heart" should rise to "this bright vision." But one wonders which vision Wheatley is referring to—the vision of resurrection or the vision of equality. Though Wheatley appears to uphold the virtues of her Christian readers through her celebration of Whitefield's career, she strategically uses the elegy to give voice to her own sermon, as she poses the moral dilemma of slavery.

Unlike many of her epistles to famous individuals of her time, Wheatley's poem "To the Right Honourable William, Earl of Dartmouth, His Majesty's Principal Secretary of State for North America, & C." briefly mentions Wheatley's position as a slave, and it is the only personal reference to her servitude. Similar to her epistle on King George, Wheatley's oblique lines of praise maintain favor in the eyes of both royalist and patriot readers. Written after the publication of her 1772 Proposals, Wheatley sings:

> Hail, happy day, when smiling like the mourn,
> Fair *Freedom* rose *New-England* to adorn:
> The northern clime beneath her genial ray,
> *Dartmouth*, congratulates thy blissful sway:
> Elate with hope her race no longer mourns,
> Each soul expands, each grateful bosom burns,
> While in thine hand with please we behold
> The silken reins, and *Freedom's* charms unfold. (Wheatley 82-3)

The reader is immediately drawn into the poem through the personification of Freedom as a "fair" and charming woman. In later lines Wheatley describes Freedom as a "Goddess" who "shines supreme" (Wheatley 83). The arbitrary use of "each soul expands" along with the pronoun "we" speaks to all readers. Wheatley seems to include herself in the "we" as well, as she gives credit to "Dartmouth" for Freedom's rise in New England. It is unclear whose hand holds "the silken reins," since it can be read as either Freedom or the earl himself, a distinction that Wheatley refuses to make in order to maintain her appeal in both London and New England. The tone of the poem can be read by royalists as praise for England's gesture to relinquish such "reins" on freedom, such as the Stamp Act. Patriot readers are able to read the tone of the poem as sympathetic to their emancipation from England. In either case, Wheatley once again guises her political motives in pre-Revolutionary politics.

The celebratory tone continues with Wheatley's ironic praise:

> No more, *America*, in mournful strains
> Of wrongs, and grievance unredress'd complain,
> No longer shalt thou dread the iron chain,
> Which wanton *Tyranny* with lawless hand
> Had made, and with it meant t' enslave the land. (Wheatley 83)

The words "iron chain," "tyranny," and "enslave" point readers indirectly to Wheatley's racialized experience as the poem speaks metaphorically to the struggle between New and Old England. What makes these lines so terribly ironic is that on the surface her praises of the earl are bittersweet when placed within the context that she herself is unable to enjoy the "genial ray" of Freedom that her readers experience.

For a fleeting moment, Wheatley removes the guise of appearing part of the readers' circle, speaking without the refined overlay of verse epistle, addressing the Earl directly:

> Should you, my lord, while you peruse my song,
> Wonder from whence my love of *Freedom* sprung,
> Whence flow these wishes for the common good,
> By feeling hearts along best understood,
> I young in life, by seeming cruel fate
> Was snatch'd from *Afric's* fancy'd happy seat:
> What pangs excruciating must molest,
> What sorrows labour in my parent's breast?
> Steel'd was that soul and by no misery mov'd
> That from a father seiz'd his babe belov'd:
> Such, such my case. And can I then but prayer
> Others may never feel tyrannic sway? (Wheatley 83)

Both the earl and the reader are reminded of her outsider status—and her captivity. Briefly, she uses her narrative as a metaphor for the captivity the colonists have felt and the overwhelming joy they feel for any amount of freedom they gain. She makes it clear that she does not enjoy that freedom, but because she does so through the use of the extended metaphor of her own captivity, she does not offend her audience. The stanza also serves as important proof that Wheatley is capable of a "feeling heart," an attribute that was presumed "incompatible with Wheatley's race" (Wilcox 25). Without the ability to feel, she can have neither the "love of Freedom" nor the "wishes for the common good" expressed in the first couple of stanzas, but this third stanza counters this presumption (Wilcox 25). As Kirsten Wilcox argues, "The story suggests that Wheatley has greater claim to a 'feeling heart' than her white readers, who are linked by their race to the captor 'steel'd . . . and by no misery mov'd'" (25). In fact, the entire stanza is almost a precursor to the convention of sentimentality indicative of the rising novel as it pulls on the heartstrings of readers through the explicit description of a child being torn from the "parent's breast." The stanza ends with an important question to her readers, as Wheatley wonders if "others may never feel tyrannic sway?" The question forces the reader to look directly at the face of slavery and feel with Wheatley "pangs excruciating."

As quickly as she removes the mask, it is once again replaced in the fourth stanza. Before the reader can get too fixed on her true identity, she returns to the ambiguity of pronoun reference:

> For favours past, great Sir, our thanks are due,
> And thee we ask thy favours to renew,
> Since in they pow'r, as in thy will before,
> To sooth the griefs, which thou did'st once deplore.
> May heav'nly grace the sacred sanction gives
> To all thy works, and thou for ever live
> Not only on the wings of fleeting *Fame,*
> Though praise immortal crowns the patriot's name,
> But to conduct to heav'ns refulgent fane,
> May fiery coursers sweep th' etheral plain,
> And bear thee upwards to that blest abode,
> Where, like the prophet, thou shalt find thy God. (Wheatley 83).

Replacing the singular "I" from the previous stanza with "we" and "our," Wheatley removes herself. The poem ends with the same tones of praise with which it began, with an offering of "thanks" to the earl for "favours past." Wheatley does remind him that he has the power to "sooth the griefs" of any future tyranny. She emphasizes that his fame is "fleeting" and that if he truly wants to be remembered, he must conduct himself with "heav'nly grace" by upholding freedom. The address to the earl serves as a type of carrier wave for Wheatley to send the same emancipatory message to her readers about their power to remove the "iron chains" of slavery.

Circulated to promote her upcoming book, as she journeyed to London to meet with publisher Archibald Bell, Wheatley's widely published poem "Farewell to America, to Mrs. S.W." is one of her most allusive expression regarding her resistance to slavery. The poem anticipates her days at sea, her arrival in London, and the restoration of her health, since she was chronically ill. The initials of the dedication refer to Susanna Wheatley. Written in quatrains, she bids her farewell:

I.
Adieu, *New-England's* smiling meads,
Adieu, the flow'ry plain:
I leave thin op'ning charms, O spring,
And tempt the roaring main.

II.
In vain for me the flow'rets rise,
And boast their gaudy pride,
While here beneath the northern skies
I mourn for *health* deny'd.

Knowing that Wheatley suffered from poor health, the reader assumes that the final line of stanza two is her hope that the salty seas and fresh air will renew her. However, when the word "health" is coupled with the verb "deny'd," it becomes apparent that Wheatley is alluding to an affliction other than her chronic illness; she is mourning her "freedom deny'd."

In the next several quatrains, Wheatley imagines the grief of her mistress, as she describes how "Susannah mourns" with "tender falling" tears "at sad departure's hour" (Wheatley 108). Capturing the landscape of New England in spring, Wheatley also imagines how she will miss the "feather'd warblers sing," "the garden blooms," and "sweet perfumes" (Wheatley 108). By stanza seven, Wheatley's attention shifts from gazing back on New England to looking forward to "Britannia's distant shore" (108). With a burst of jubilation, Wheatley exclaims:

VIII.
Lo! *Health* appears! celestial dame!
Complacent and serene,
With *Hebe's* mantle o'er her Fame,
With soul-delighting mein.

Health becomes a personified figure, similar to Freedom in the address to the earl. At the first glance of British shoreline, which she attributes to "health," the tone of the poem becomes impatient. Wheatley complains, "Why, *Phoebus,* moves the cart to slow?" (Wheatley 109). By the ninth quatrain, Wheatley expresses sudden conflicted feelings:

XI.
For thee, *Brittania*, I resign
New-England's smiling fields;
To view again her charms divine,
What joy the prospect yields!

The expression of elation mixed with homesickness would be a normal response for a young girl who had never traveled far from home. Readers could easily connect with the emotional farewell and the joy of reaching the final destination.

Yet for Wheatley these conflicted feelings are much deeper, because for her "Brittania" is "freedom," and she knows that if she is going to be relieved of the afflictions of slavery, she may never return to New England. A British case involving a black slave named James Somerset set a new precedent for black slaves enslaved in Britain, and it offered the possibility of asylum for slaves that were to be transported from England against their will (Davis 497-98). The Somerset case caused controversy, especially in Boston, where it was the subject of press publications, commentary, and editorial reactions. Two Boston newspapers reported the fear of an English correspondent that "these black Gentry will visit us in too great an abundance, intermarry with our women, and thus in time we shall become a Nation of Molattoes" (Wilcox 7). Miscellaneous anecdotes from the trial ran in three Boston weeklies from late July 1772, when a report of this "remarkable Cause pending in the Court of King's Bench" appeared in the *Massachusetts Gazette and Boston Weekly News-Letter*, through mid-October (Wilcox 5). The decision of the judge, Lord Mansfield, confirmed the spurious legal maxim that "as soon as a Negro slave comes into England he becomes *free*" (Davis 469-501). With such clamor circulating about Boston, Wheatley surely must have heard about the Somerset case would certainly have understood the implications of it for herself.

Though the last two stanzas may be read as an "apostrophe to Temptation," in an "effort to find religious significance in the mixed emotions prompted by the prospect of a long voyage," when the historical context of the Somerset case is taken into consideration, the poem presents a specific "temptation" for Wheatley (Wilcox 4). Wheatley exclaims:

> XII.
> But thou! Temptation hence away,
> With all thy fatal train
> Nor once seduce my soul away,
> By thine enchanting strain.

> XIII.
> Thrice happy they, whose heav'nly shield
> Secures their souls from harms,
> And fell *Temptation* on the fields
> Of all is pow'r disarms! (Wheatley 109)

Although it appears that Wheatley is adhering to her religious convictions, the poem's piety hides the real "disarming" temptation for Wheatley—to stay on British soil where her "health," her "freedom," will be "secured" from "harm."

Phillis Wheatley never enjoyed the possibilities she longs for in her "Farewell to America." As preparations for the book's publication were become finalized, Wheatley received a message that Susanna Wheatley was seriously ill. Torn between her desire to stay and the wish to tend to her dying mistress, Wheatley decided to return to Boston. Her sudden change of plans caused her to refuse an invitation to visit the Countess of Huntingdon in Wales and to forego meeting the king. Wheatley sailed for New England near the end of July, arriving in Boston on September 13, 1773. Although her book was published in early September 1773, Wheatley did not receive the first copies of it until January 1774 (Mason 8). Immediately upon receiving the copies, she began marketing them in letters and in person while caring for her dying mistress. On March 3, 1774, Susanna Wheatley died, leaving Phillis to fend for herself. Apparently she was allowed to reside in the Wheatley home with Mr. Wheatley as long as he was able to live there. Both children had long since married and moved away. It would have seemed that freedom would be unattainable now that she was back in Boston, but sometime between September 13 and October 18 Wheatley was freed by her master (Mason 8).

III. "IN VAIN THE FEATHER'D WARBLERS SING"

On October 18, 1773, Phillis Wheatley wrote Col. David Worcester:

> —Since my return to America my Master, has at the desire of my friends in England given me my freedom, The Instrument is drawn, so as to secure me and my property from the hands of the Executers, administrators, &c. of my master, & secure whatsoever Should be given me as my Own, a copy is Sent to Isra. Mauduit Esqr. F.R.S. (Wheatley 197)

Wheatley obtained her long-sought freedom through the written word. Proving that she was capable of expression within the marketplace, readers were forced to reexamine their own preconceptions. Nor would she have been able to gain such agency with her audiences. By carefully constructing her poems, she managed to appeal to her white readership, while covertly espousing her own politics.

As Barbara Johnson suggests, Wheatley's poems worked on her audience like puzzles, as readers asked themselves, "What's wrong with this picture?" (Johnson 196-7). Wheatley made certain that the puzzle appeared to be theirs and not her own (Willard 243). Projecting a passive persona that mirrored the religious values and political ideologies of her readers, and in the gaps of silence produced by her use of arbitrariness, Wheatley created a discursive space to express herself, ultimately gaining enough agency to obtain manumission. She understood that "freedom in the form of manumission or a privileged status was the reward for those considered acceptably accultured" (Bell 173).

Wheatley fashioned herself and her poetics, dressing in pre-Revolutionary metaphors to "sell" herself to both royalist and patriot readers. In many ways, using the struggle over geography, economics, and freedom of expression was germane to her own plight because as a slave, she was relegated to the position of property. The process of cultural assimilation, the prize of precious few during Wheatley's day, leads to what W.E.B. DuBois later describes in *The Souls of Black Folks* as a:

> peculiar sensation, this double-consciousness, this sense of always looking at one's self through the eyes of others, of measuring one's soul by the tape of a world that looks on in amused contempt and pity. One ever feels his twoness,—an American, a Negro; two souls, two thoughts, two unrecoiled strivings; two warring ideals in one dark body, whose dogged strength alone keeps it from being torn asunder (XXX)

Black slaves were among the first colonists to build a nation, yet that nation denied them freedom. All slaves were "destined to function on two levels of reality, and their attitudes toward integration and separatism were largely determined by the degree of alienation from or faith in the principles of the dominant white Anglo-Saxon Protestant society" (Bell 173).

Wheatley assimilated herself into the dominant eighteenth-century conceptions of authorship, and by gaining the sympathies of her vast readership, whose published responses chided the Wheatley family for keeping the poet a slave, forced the Wheatley family to free her (Isani 144-9). But freedom from slavery did not mean freedom from oppression for Wheatley. The historian Edmund Morgan writes that one of the most powerful, unifying features of nationalizing discourse was, in fact, the difference maintained between poor tenant-farming whites and newly freed African American slaves (363-441). The category of "common" sense and "common" man, proliferated by Revolutionary thinkers such as Thomas Paine, excluded individuals like Wheatley, causing racial division and ambivalence in the newly forming democracy. Although a slave could enjoy "freedom," it did not entitle a slave to enjoy democracy." For the poor classes, "freedom" could mean "upward mobility"; for the slave population it meant continued containment (Morgan 363-441).

So it was for Phillis Wheatley, whose life after 1776 steadily moved toward poverty and oblivion (Willard 248). With the political tide turning during the outbreak of the Revolutionary War, colonists focused on raising troops and funding a war against England. After the war, inflation skyrocketed, making books an impossible commodity to sell. Abroad, the taste of British citizens soured toward anything remotely related to the American colonies. Wheatley was left without support on either side of the Atlantic. After the death of Mr. Wheatley, Phillis was left nothing in his will, and his two children offered no support. Wheatley was forced to etch out an abject existence for herself and her family at a black boardinghouse in Boston. None of her former friends or powerful readers came to her rescue and none attended her funeral (Robinson 60-65). Upon her death in 1784, Phillis's husband sold the remaining copies of her now unmarketable book, along with the beautifully bound volumes of Pope and Milton that she had received as gifts during her trip to London.

Her 1779 list of proposals indicates that she continued to write throughout the Revolutionary years during the sickness that claimed the lives of her three children, her own chronic illness, and her extremely unhappy marriage. The second proposed volume, dedicated to Benjamin Franklin, never materialized. Wheatley's voice was silenced. When reading her 1784 "Elegy on Leaving," one of her last poems, where she faces her own imminent death, it is hard not to see the irony of her emancipation. In many ways she had more freedom as a Wheatley slave, since in that discursive space she was able to adapt to traditional conventions of neoclassical expression, becoming the "unexpected genius" that offered her such notoriety in the marketplace that she was able to freely walk in circles that most of her readers were unable to appreciate. Fame provided Wheatley with a passage to freedom, but freedom did not offer her the means to elevate herself from the "iron chains" of the hostile world that arguably made all of her poetic efforts vain.

Conclusion
Remember the Ladies: Female
Poets in Nineteenth-Century America

We may not "cry aloud," as they are bid,
And lift our voices in the "public" ear;
Nor yet be mute. The pen is ours to wield,
The heart to will, and hands to execute.

—Eliza Earle, 1837

In the war for America's political independence, the final battle with the British ended when Cornwallis withdrew his army to the tip of the Virginia peninsula between the York and James rivers. There, General Washington quickly advanced over seven thousand troops southward, and with the aid of the Comte de Grasse, who brought a French fleet from the West Indies, forced a British surrender on October 1781. In November 1782, a preliminary peace agreement was reached in Paris; it was formally signed in September 1783. The war was finally over. America had finally become a free and sovereign nation.

The independent colonists faced the enormous task of deciding how the new nation would be governed. The years immediately following the end of the Revolution were extremely difficult. Over half of the total population was under sixteen years of age. Terrible inflation and a postwar economic depression created restlessness and tension among the newly independent colonists. The government established under the Articles of Confederation in 1781 failed to effectively unify the states. As a result, a meeting was held in Philadelphia in 1787 to draft a new constitution, one that would base its authority on "We the People."

Throughout the constitutional era, the primary challenge for post-Revolutionary America was to decide how to define it's self. Both male and female writers desired to create a new literature that was at once unique and reflective of the new United States. Writers such as Emerson, Thoreau, Wadsworth, and Whitman wanted to create a truly "American" literature. Thus Sarah Margaret Fuller writes in her famous 1846 essay surveying American literature:

> For it does not follow because many books are written by persons born in America that there exists an American literature. Books which imitate or represent the thoughts and life of Europe do not constitute an American literature. Before such can exist, an original idea must animate this nation and fresh currents of life must call into life fresh thoughts along its shore. (Fuller 134)

Independence from England created an opportunity for a "Renaissance" of new, "American" ideas. Early to mid-Nineteenth-century writers worked to create a national literature that reflected the originality and "freshness" of a new nation.

Historically disenfranchised groups saw this new era as an opportunity to be recognized as participating citizens. And historically marginalized writers saw this as an opportunity to contribute to a new national literature. Women, slaves, and ex-slaves saw the creation of a new constitution as a vehicle for finally becoming part of "We the People," in particular, as Abigail Adams had once bid her husband to "Remember the Ladies," women began claiming their right to have a public voice.

Unfortunately, the U.S. Constitution, which was ratified in 1788, and the inauguration of George Washington as the first president demonstrated that "We the People" did not necessarily include minority members of society. It would take more than a century for women to gain the legal right to vote. Regardless of the law, women managed to claim agency within a society that refused to recognize their full rights to citizenship. Despite custom and law, women writers contributed to the formation of a new "American" identity.

While the newly ratified constitution failed to offer women the platform from which to exercise their rights as citizens, technology and the changing infrastructure of society offered ways in which women could express their ideas publicly. Because of the economy, books were scarce, as were the means and materials to produce such an expensive commodity. Most pre-Revolutionary books in America were produced in England, and with the recent break from trade with England, the United States needed a new form of publication that was cheap and easy to print. The number of newspapers and broadsides increased in post-Revolutionary America, as did serial journal publication. The printing technology that produced media such as newspapers became more efficient and capable of quickly printing massive amounts of material for distribution. High-quality paper was extremely expensive following the war, and since newspapers and other types of print did not require such paper, these types of print materials became evermore popular.

The surge in population growth at the end of the eighteenth century and the beginning of the nineteenth century led to a greater demand for reading material that could be printed quickly and inexpensively. At the turn of the nineteenth century the new nation consisted of sixteen states, but by 1853 the United States had more than tripled in size. The Louisiana Purchase along with the Gadsden Purchase in 1853 expanded new territories for American citizens to seek opportunity. In the first half of the nineteenth century, the population more than quadrupled from 5.3 million to almost 24 million. The huge population growth generated new audiences for newspapers, magazines, and other print media. The number of newspapers increased significantly from just 200 at the turn of the century to well over 1,200 by 1830. New York City alone had 47 newspapers.

Along with the surge in population growth, the establishment of a public school system further fostered the demand for more print material. Prior to the American Revolution, education had been available to only the upper class, and within that class men were the primary recipients of education. Following the Revolution there were two very important educational changes in education that took place. First, states became willing to fund elementary schools from tax monies, and second, schooling was improved for girls. Girls who received an education at the end of the eighteenth century became the literate mothers of the beginning of the nineteenth century. For the first time, the United States became one of the most literate populations in the world, and women were being given the new opportunities to attend school and become literate.

Not only were increasing numbers of women becoming more educated, they suddenly had more leisure time as the production of many household goods moved out of the home around the turn of the century. Instead household goods were becoming more available at local general stores. White middle-class women, especially in the North, were able to become participants in the public marketplace. They constituted a new, large consumer base and purchased reading material, among other things. This new audience of readers provided an ideal way for writers, especially fiction writers, to support themselves. Women also became active in social reform movements, including the women's rights movement, which held its first formal convention in Seneca Falls, New York, in 1848. In many ways the nineteenth century afforded American women with more intellectual freedom than ever before.

However, American women in many ways found their sphere more narrowly defined than it had been in previous centuries. Their ability to control property, vote, and run for office was nonexistent. Women were increasingly expected to devote themselves to the domestic sphere as the "angel in the house." Women were expected to stay home and only orient their lives around the well-being of their family, providing a moral example to their children. Their lives often became trivialized, isolated, and restricted by custom and law. Yet female consumers were a major force that moved and defined nineteenth-century America. While custom and law may have limited women from certain aspects of cultural participation, they found agency by writing and reading each other's published material. As Mary E. Bryan describes in "How Should Women Write?" written in 1860:

> Men, after much demure and hesitation have given women liberty to write; but, they can not consent to allow them full freedom. They may flutter out of the cage, but it must be with clipped wings; they may hop about the smooth-shaven lawn, but must, on no account, fly. With metaphysics they have nothing to do; it is too deep a sea for their lead to sound; nor must they grapple with those great social and moral problems with which every strong soul is now wrestling. They must not go beyond the surface of life, lest they should stir the impure sediment that lurks beneath. . . . Having prescribed these bounds to the female pen, men are the first to condemn her efforts as tame and commonplace, because they lack earnestness and strength.

Bryan's complaint is indicative of the plight of the female writer in nineteenth-century America. Many women were forced to focus on subjects and adopt strategies that were different than those employed by men. While still just as "serious" and "popular" as their male counterparts, women writers of the nineteenth century reflect the differing conditions in which they participated and were defined by American culture.

To adequately examine the history of literary production in early America and understand the ways in which women poets "made it", it is important to carry this study into the nineteenth century. It is important because the conditions in which women worked in post-Revolutionary America are vastly different than they were in seventeenth- and eighteenth-century America. According to Davis and Joyce's bibliographical survey, *Poetry by Women to 1900*, only 18 American female poets published volumes of poetry before 1800, as opposed to 210 in Britain. During the nineteenth century, 1,609 volumes of poetry were published by women writers, and by the last half of the nineteenth century, American female poets out-produced their transatlantic rivals. Women writers had definitely become a force in literary America. In the introduction to *The Female Poets of America*, published in 1849, Rufus W. Griswold describes the magnitude of female verse:

> The most striking quality of that civilization which is evolving itself in America, is the deference felt for women. As a point in social manners, it is so pervading and so peculiar, as to amount to a national characteristic. . . . The increased degree in which women among us are taking a leading part in literature, is one

of the circumstances of this augmented distinction. . . . The proportion of female writers at this moment in America, far exceeds that which the present or any other age in England exhibits. (8)

A combination of technological and economic changes regarding in printing allowed women to claim agency in the public marketplace in a way that had not been possible before the early 1800s. Basic printing processes from papermaking and typesetting to the press technology itself became fully mechanized by the 1830s, and the new railroads led to more expansive and mechanized methods of distribution. Women were no longer limited to social networks to reach audiences, but could use technology to distribute to a wider readership. The mechanization of processes resulted in cheaper products, which in turn helped create a mass market. It became easy to sell a book or other printed material, because the mass market, which included mostly middle-class America, could afford reading material that had once been available to only the elite class. By the 1830s, "following the early lead of tract and bible stories, major publishers began to issue low-cost books in paperbound and serial format aimed at a wide range of readers, with particularly precipitous price drops occasioned by the economic crises of the late 1820's" (Martin 437-8).

The mass market of the nineteenth century led to new ways in which culture was configured as a result of the various methods to reprint, anthologize, and illustrate text. By the end of the first third of the nineteenth century, almost all publishers on both sides of the Atlantic "refused to publish the generic marker of High Romanticism—stand-alone volumes of poetry"—as a result all sales shifted suddenly to new mixed forms, particularly multivolume 'libraries,' illustrated literary annuals, and gift-book anthologies (Siskin 12; Martin 438).

In fact, women's poetry in the United States between 1800 and 1850 can be broken down into two distinct periods. During the first two and a half decades of the new century, women poets continued using newspapers and periodicals as their primary venues of public discourse, publishing as few as forty-five books (Bennett 28). This poetry has more in common stylistically with eighteenth-century verse than with the poetry penned by the following generation of "literary domestics" or "sentimentalists." As Bennett describes, "It remains a poetry of wit and cultural debate, varied by odes to nature or poems dedicated to historical personages or events" (28). However, after the mid-1820s the number of poetry volumes by American women escalated. During this period "women began to adopt the affect-based style enjoined on them both by sentimental literature and by their new roles as domestic saviors, incipient municipal housekeepers, and 'Angels in the House'" (Bennett 28).

Of the many female poets writing in America during the first half of the nineteenth century, including Elizabeth Oakes, Sarah Wentworth Apthorp

Morton, Frances Sargent Osgood, and Susan Hale, the woman who best represents the changing mass market is Lydia Huntley Sigourney. Although she was hardly anthologized in the twentieth century and is only now being re-examined for her merit, Sigourney was one of the most popular writers of nineteenth-century America. Sigourney can be credited with setting the pattern for women's poetry, a pattern that remained unchallenged for more than a century. Sigourney's career is significant because it illustrates how a woman "made" it as a writer. Sigourney, like many of the women poets in the early nineteenth century, came from a poor home; her father was a gardener. To provide financial support for her ill parents, Sigourney worked from 1811 to 1819 operating a school for young women in Norwich and Hartford, Connecticut. During her years as an educator, Sigourney published her first work, *Moral Pieces in Prose and Verse*, in 1815. She was an instant success.

Hailed as the "American Hemans," the "Sweet Singer of Hartford," and a "female Milton," Huntley was more popular than many of her male counterparts. She continued to publish several editions of *Moral Pieces*, along with a large quantity of poems and prose pieces. Until her marriage in 1833, Sigourney published her work under her own name. Her husband, a hardware merchant, bank president, and college trustee, felt that his position might be injured if the public knew that his wife was a poet (Haight 35). Only after his fortunes failed in the early 1830s did Sigourney return to using her own name again. It became imperative for her to write to support the family, and by using her own name, her early notoriety as a writer quickly helped rejuvenate her career. Although the years following 1830 were her most prosperous, her anonymity during the first part of her marriage gave her great freedom to explore a range of topics and themes in her poetry. Sigourney's success further flourished beyond her poetry. In 1837 Sigourney and Sarah Josepha Hale were chosen as the two vice presidents for the Willard Association for the Mutual Improvement of Female Teachers. Hale was the editor of the recently merged *Ladies Magazine* and *Godey's Lady's Book*. The merger produced the most influential women's magazines of the era, shaping a range of trends from women's rights to women's fashions, and offered further opportunities for male and female writers. The contributors included Emerson, Longfellow, Poe, and Stowe, as well as many lesser-known women authors. The relationship between Sigourney and Hale provided the necessary venue for networking with other major writers of her era. Sigourney also wrote an introductory preface to one of Felicia Hemans's works, endorsing Hemans's poetry, despite the fact that some accused Sigourney of imitation.

When examining the career of Lydia Huntley Sigourney and the ways in which she "made it" as a poet, one finds that her strategies for gaining agency are similar to those of Anne Bradstreet and Phillis Wheatley; social connections also launched her writing career. Walking in the elite circles of Hartford, the Wadsworth family financially supported Sigourney and urged her not only to start a girls school in Hartford, which they helped fund, but also to publish her first work of poetry. Through their family connections, *Moral Pieces* became the first of over fifty volumes she would publish during her lifetime. *Moral Pieces* was so popular that advance subscriptions numbering nearly a thousand copies (selling for a dollar each) immediately required a reprinting. Much of the flurry surrounding the publication can be attributed to Mr. Wadsworth's desire to further her career. In fact, Wadsworth read all the proof and edited the work, along with writing the prefatory material, insisting that it include an explanation to the reader that Miss Sigourney was a self-made poet. He wrote in a letter to her:

> After writing two or three little things by way of Preface—your Friends here all agree that on the one [?] following, the most simple, & short, of the whole, will be proper & all that is requisite.—Nothing would be necessary but for the purpose of letting the Public know, that the Author has not had the advantages of Affluence, & *a life of education*, among those, whose literary taste, knowledge for the world, & elegant accomplishments, might render her acquirements only a matter of course.—This simple statement of facts, will I think, without the appearance of asking forbearance, soften criticism. It is but justice to yourself, that the Public should have some sense of how entirely all you possess of literature has been from your own exertions. (Haight 12)

By situating herself as a self-made writer, she upholds the American myth that anyone can "make it" in the new nation if she exerts enough will. Although she may not have possessed rights equal to those of her male counterparts, her success as a self-made writer demonstrates that women are just as capable of claiming a voice in the formation of a new "American" identity.

Similar to Bradstreet and Wheatley, Sigourney adjusted her poetics to fit her readers' tastes, and by doing so she was able to espouse her own political agenda without offending her audience. Though she was severely criticized both in her own day and by twentieth-century critics as being overly trite, sentimental, and repetitive, her work and career reflect a woman who carefully constructed her poetry to gain popularity while still exploring political topics that many writers avoided. Roy Pearce harshly comments, "Below [the Fireside poets] were other poets, Mrs. Sigourney and her kind, who, lacking intelligence to assume their proper responsibilities, catered to and exploited the general (or generalized) reader" (197). Jay Hubbell complains that Sigourney and other poets such as Hemans "helped greatly to popularize a kind of debased Romanticism among readers who did not care for the far greater poems of Wordsworth, Shelley, and Keats" (608). Nina Baym describes the base stereotyping of Sigourney as a result of "a succession of audiences, each basing its commentary and opinion on an ever smaller portion of original record" (387). Baym summarizes:

> Even now, when writing by antebellum American women is more highly valued than it has been for a long time, the mere mention of Sigourney's name suffices to invoke a caricature: a mildly comical figure who exemplifies the worst aspects of domestic sentimentalism. (387)

Baym argues, however, that while Sigourney did write an enormous number of occasional poems, consolation elegies, and funerary pieces, her work constitutes a large and important piece of literary history.

Some of the harshest contemporary criticism was written by fellow poet Edgar Allen Poe. In 1835, as editor of the *Southern Literary Messenger*, Poe's contempt for the shameless puffing by which the literary *Epizoeas* showed as he called them, succeeded "in creating for themselves as absolutely positive reputation, by mere dint of the continuity and perpetuity of their appeals to the public" (7). Poe had a mania for finding resemblances, even when none existed, and to him referring to Sigourney as "the American Hemans" was tantamount to an accusation of plagiarism (Haight 79). Reviewing Mrs. Sigourney's *Zinzendorff and Other Poems* in the *Messenger* for January 1836 he writes:

> Mrs. Sigourney has long been known as an author. Her earliest publication was reviewed about twenty years ago in the North America. . . . The fame she has since acquired is extensive; and we, who so much admire her virtues and her talents, and who have so frequently expressed our admiration of both this Journal—we, of all persons—are the least inclined to call in question the justice or accuracy of the public opinion, by which has been adjudged to her so high a station among the *literati* of our land. Some things, however, we cannot pass over in silence. There are two kinds of popular reputation,—or rather there are two roads by which such reputation may be attainted. . . . Let us suppose two writers having a reputation apparently equal—that is to say their names *being equally in the mouths of the people*. . . . The one has written a great work. . . . And let us imagine that, by this single effort, the author has attained a certain quantum of reputation. We know it to be possible that another writer of very moderate powers may build up for himself, little by little, a reputation equally great—and, this too, merely by keeping continually in the eye, or by appealing continually with little things, to the ear, of that great, overgrown, and majestical gander, the critical and bibliographical rabble.
>
> It would be easy, although perhaps a somewhat disagreeable task, to point out several of the most popular writers in America—popular in the above mentioned sense—who have manufactured for themselves a celebrity by the very questionable manner, to which we have alluded. But it must not be thought that we wish to include Mrs. Sigourney in the number. By no means. She has trod,

however, upon the confines of their circle. She does not *owe* her reputation to the chicanery we mention, but it cannot be denied that it has been thereby greatly assisted. In a word—no single piece which she has written, and not even her collected works as we behold them in the present volume, and in the one published some years ago, would fairly entitle her to that exalted rank which she actually enjoys as the authoress, *time after time*, of her numerous, and in most instances, very creditable compositions. (12)

Later in the review Poe speaks specifically about Sigourney's title of the "American Hemans," commenting that "Mrs. S. cannot conceal from her own discernment that she has acquired this title *solely by imitation*. The very phrase 'American Hemans' speaks loudly in accusation" (12). Poe then judiciously condemns, "We will briefly point out the particulars in which Mrs. Sigourney stands palpably convicted of that sin which in poetry is not to be forgiven." (12)

For Poe, or anyone else, to accuse Sigourney of plagiarism is a misrepresentation of her popularity. When reading the body of her work, it becomes apparent that like many writers of the nineteenth century who lived on the money they made, she wrote too much too fast. Often her poems needed reworking and editing. In many instances she ran out of topics and tended to repeat herself, a problem many eighteenth-century elegists experienced. As Watts sympathetically explains, "Especially when her family's meals depended on her pen (after 1832), her poems were padded, pedantic, and prudish" (84). Nowhere, however, does she plagiarize. Like many poets, she imitated the poetic style of authors, which included the work of Cowper, Hannah Moore, Wordsworth, and Byron (Haight 77-79). As Watts comments, "Her 'imitation' was that of an independent poet, who may have drawn thematic inspiration from the other poets, who did in fact learn prosodic techniques from the other poets, but whose thematic and image development was clearly her own" (84).

In the context of my argument, what becomes interesting in examining Sigourney is that in many ways Poe's comments, while overly accusatory, do have some credibility. Although Sigourney did not plagiarize and was thematically innovative, she did have a good sense of what the market demanded in terms of producing a commodity that people wanted to read. And she "packaged" her themes to make them acceptable to her readership. Like women writers in the centuries before her, Sigourney carefully constructed her poetry to fit within the prescribed role for writers, especially women writers of the early to mid-nineteenth century, while at the same time working within those boundaries to publish her own ideas. Like nearly all poets of the nineteenth century, Sigourney wrote about death; many of her poems are elegies. In the 1834 edition of her work, most of the subjects are dead mothers and their children.

Yet, in comparison to her contemporaries, while she did reiterate this form repeatedly, she used the elegy for various poetic investigations. Her work examines a variety of concerns, including the plight of the Indians, slaves, and temperance, along with blind and deaf children. Even as she wrote about women and children, her poetry captured them as real people who were not to be dismissed as unimportant. As Watt explains, "On the most simple level, Sigourney was attempting to deal honestly and in fairly real terms with the emotions, frustrations, and tragedies of the deaths of real children and their real mothers." Unlike many of her contemporaries, "She was simply not satisfied with the general thought that we all die" (86). In broader terms, Sigourney's poetry was very democratic in her portrayal of women and children. While the majority of the dead children and mothers in her poetry are identical, just as many of her poems are identical in style and pattern, the repetitive similarity of all the subjects demonstrates the American ideal that they are all identical because they are all "American" mothers and children. As Watt states:

> If there is anything really American in the more broad philosophical sense in her poetry, it is this democratic tendency: her realization that the death of those who have "achieved" nothing or who are part of the mass (not even the humble beggar of Wordsworth's poems) is as important as the death of ministers, queens, civic leaders, heroes, or even fathers. (87)

The democratic quality of her subjects makes her a poetic pioneer who employs the overused genre of the elegy to advance her own view of what it meant to be a mother or child in nineteenth-century America.

Along with her progressive view of mothers and children, Sigourney's poetry is filled with a profound concern for family, with each member, even the tiniest baby, as observed in "'Twas But a Babe." Although the poetry of Bradstreet and Wheatley display infants and children as appropriate subject matter for serious poetry, it was Sigourney who repeatedly put significance on the family—an ideal important to the concept of "America." Another radical difference in Sigourney's work is her concern for fathers. In most of the poetry by American women after 1800, men as fathers are almost totally absent (Watt 87). Although a man's voice may be muted or he may feel the "poverty of speech," the father is almost always present. It is Sigourney's poetry that edifies the American ideal that every member of the family is important, even the women. The loss of a mother and wife is a loss for society in her elegies because it is the woman who is the spiritual guide, comforter, and teacher—a role fathers do not achieve. Sigourney illustrates that the American woman, though relegated to the domestic sphere, is equal to the American man in the public sphere. The importance of continuing this study to include Sigourney therefore lies in the fact that her poetry advocates a more equal and honest view of women's contribution to the formation of the new nation.

By tracing the poetic strategies of these three American women writers over the course of nearly three hundred years, one sees how complex and self-conscious they were about their authorial construction, as they struggled to make sure that they worked within their prescribed roles as women. Despite the rapid changes in technology, print distribution, and the transforming political climate of early America, the ways in which these women negotiated their roles as wives, mothers, and writers does not change. Each worked from within her prescribed role and found ways to claim a voice for herself, moving her own political agenda forward. All three refused to sit in silence or on the margins of society. Instead they found clever ways to write themselves into the text of America, and in doing so helped shape a piece of American history. By their own movement, they claimed the right to write.

Works Cited

Achinstein, Sharon. *Milton and the Revolutionary Reader*. Princeton, NJ: Princeton UP, 1994.

Adair, John Eric. *Puritans: Religion and Politics in Seventeenth Century England and America.* Gloucestershire: Sutton Publishing Limited, 1998.

Baraka, Amiri. *Daggers and Javelins: Essays, 1974-1979*. NY: William Morrow, 1984.

Baym, Nina. "Reinventing Lydia Sigourney." *American Literature*, 62. Sept. 1990. 385-404.

Bell, Bernard. "African-American Writers." *American Literature: 1764-1789 The Revolutionary Years*. Ed. Everett Emerson. Madison, WI: U of Wisconsin P, 1977.

Bennett, H.S. *English Books and Readers 1558-1603*. Cambridge: Cambridge UP, 1965.

Bradstreet, Anne. *The Tenth Muse: and from the Manuscripts, Meditations Divine and Morall together with Letters and Occasional Pieces*. Intro. Josephine K. Piercy. Gainesville, Florida: Scholars' Facsimiles & Reprints, 1965.

Bradstreet, Anne. *The Works of Anne Bradstreet: In Prose and Verse*. ed. John Harvard Ellis. New York: Peter Smith, 1932.

Cappon, Lester J., ed. *The Adams-Jefferson Letters: The Complete Correspondence Between Thomas Jefferson and Abigail and John Adams*. 2 vols. NY: Simon and Schuster, 1971.

Chartier, Roger. *The Order of Books: Readers, Authors, and Libraries in Europe between the Fourteenth and Eighteenth Centuries*. Trans. Lydia G. Cochrane. Stanford: Stanford UP, 1994.

Clair, Colin. *A History of Printing in Britain*. New York: Oxford UP, 1966.

Countryman, Edward. *The American Revolution*. NY: Hill and Wang, 1985.

Davis, Gwen. *Poetry by Women to 1900: a Bibliography of American and British Writers*. London & NY: Mansell, 1991.

Donne, John. *Bianthanatos*. Ed. Ernest W. Sullivan II. Newark, NJ, 1984.

Dubois, W.E.B. *The Souls of Black Folks*. Intro. Herb Boyd. NY: Random House, 1996.

Eisenstein, Elizabeth. *The Printing Press as as Agent of Change*. Cambridge: Cambridge UP, 1980.

Elliot, Emory. "The Development of the Puritan Funeral Sermon and Elegy: 1650-1750." *Early American Literature* 15, 1980. 151-64.

Emerson, Everett. "The Cultural Context of the American Revolution." *American Literature: 1764-1789 The Revolutionary Years*. Madison, WI: U of Wisconsin P, 1977.

Ezell, Margaret J. M. *Social Authorship and the Advent of Print*. Baltimore & London: Johns Hopkins UP, 1999.

Feather, John P. "The Book in History and the History of the Book." *The History of Books and Libraries: Two Views*. Ed. John P. Feather and David McKitterick. Washington D.C.: Smithsonian Institution P, 1986.

Ferguson, Robert. *Reading and the Early Republic*. Cambridge, Mass: Harvard UP, 2004.

Finch, Anne. *The Poems of Anne Countess of Winchilsea*. Ed. Myra Reynolds. Chicago: U of Chicago P, 1903.

Foster, Frances Smith. *Written By Herself: Literary Production by African American Women, 1746-1892*. Bloomington, IN: Indiana UP, 1993.

Franklin, John Hope. *From Slavery to Freedom: A History of Negro Americans*, 4th ed. NY: Knopf, 1974.

Friedman, Jerome. *Blasphemy, Immorality, and Anarchy: The Ranters and the English Revolution*. Athens, OH: Ohio UP, 1987.

Furet, Francois. *In the Workshop of History*. Trans. Jonathan Mandelbaum. Chicago: U of Chicago Press, 1984.

Gates, Jr., Henry Louis. *The Trials of Phillis Wheatley: America's First Black Poet and Her Encounters with the Founding Fathers*. New York: Basic Civitas Books, 2003.

Gilmore, Michael. *Romanticism and the Marketplace*. Chicago: U of Chicago P, 1985.

Gregg, W. W. *Licensers for the Press, to 1640*. Oxford, 1962.

Gordon, Scott Paul. *The Power of the Passive Self in English Literature, 1640-1770*. Cambridge: Cambridge UP, 2002.

Greenblatt, Stephen. *Renaissance Self-Fashioning: From More to Shakespeare.* Chicago:U of Chicago P, 1980.

Grimstead, David. "Anglo-American Racism and Phillis Wheatley's 'Sable Veil,' 'Length'ned Chain,' and 'Knitted Heart,'" *Women in the Age of the American Revolution*. Ed. Ronald Hoffman and Peter J. Albert. Charlottesville: U of Virgina P, 1989.

Griswold, Rufus W. *The Female Poets of America*. 2nd ed. Philadelphia: Carey and Hart,1849.

Haight, Gordon S. *Mrs. Sigourney: The Sweet Singer of Hartford*. New Haven: Yale UP, 1930.

Hall, Catherine. *Family Fortunes: Men and Women of the English Middle Class, 1780-1850*. Chicago: U of Chicago P, 1987.

Hall, David. ed. *The Antinomian Controversy, 1636-1638: A Documentary History.* Middletown, Conn.:Wesleyan UP, 1968.

Hensley, Jennine. ed. *The Works of Anne Bradstreet.* Foreword Adrienne Rich. Cambridge, Mass: Belknap P of Harvard UP, 1967.

Hobby, Elaine. *Virtue of Necessity: English Women's Writing 1649-1688.* London: 1988.

Johnson, Barbara E. "Euphemism, Understatement, and the African in the Writings of Phillis Wheatley." *MELUS 6,* 1979.

Kaplain, Sidney. *The Black Presence in the Era of the American Revolution: 1770-1800.* Amherst: U of Mass. P, 1989.

Kernan, Alvin. *Samuel Johnson and the Impact of Print.* Princeton: Princeton UP, 1987.

Lang, Amy Schrager. *Prophetic Women: Anne Hutchinson and the Problem of Dissent in the Literature of New England.* Berkeley: U of California P, 1987.

Love, Harold. *Scribal Publication in Seventeenth-Century England.* Oxford: Clarendon P, 1993.

Lovelace, Richard. *The Poems of Richard Lovelace.* Ed. CH. Wilkinson. Oxford 1953.

Martin, Wendy. *An American Tryptych: Anne Bradstreet, Emily Dickinson, Adrienne Rich.* Chapel Hill: U of North Carolina P, 1984.

Mason, Julian D. *The Poems of Phillis Wheatley.* Chapel Hill: U of North Carolina P, 1989.

Morgan, Edmund S. *The Puritan Dilemma: The Story of John Winthrop.* Boston: Little, Brown, 1958.

Mulford, Carla. "Benjamin Franklin and the Myths of Nationhood," *Making America/ Making American Literature: Franklin to Cooper.* Ed. A. Robert Lee and W. M. Verhoeven.

Nord, David Paul. "A Republican Literature: Magazine Reading and Readers in Late-Eighteenth Century New York," *Reading in America: Literature and Social History.* Ed. Cathy N. Davidson. Baltimore and London: Johns Hopkins UP, 1989.

Pask, Kevin. *The Emergence of the English Author: Scripting the Life of the Poet in Early Modern England,* Cambridge and NY: Cambridge UP, 1996.

Patterson, Annabel. *Censorship and Interpretation: the Condition of Writing and Reading in Early Modern England.* Madison, WI, 1984.

Pearce, Roy Harvey. *The Continuity of American Poetry.* Princeton: Princeton UP, 1971.

Peters, Julie Stone. *Congreve, the Drama, and the Printed Word.* Stanford: Stanford UP, 1990.

Potter, Lois. *Secret Rites and Secret Writing: Royalist Literature,* 1641-1660, Cambridge. 1989

Piercy, Josephine K. *Anne Bradstreet.* New York: Twayne Publishers, Inc., 1965.

The Poems of Lady Mary Wroth. Ed. Josephine A Roberts. Baton Rouge, LA, 1983.

Robinson, William H. *Phillis Wheatley and Her Writings.* NY and London: Garland Publishing, Inc., 1984.

Rosenmeir, Rosamond. *Anne Bradstreet Revisted.* Boston: Twayne Publishers, 1991.

Round, Phillip H. *By Nature and By Custom Cursed: Transatlantic Civil Discourse and New England Cultural Production, 1620-1660*. Hanover, NH: UP of New England, 1999.

Siebert, Donald. *The Moral Animus of David Hume*. Newark: U of Delaware P, 1990.

Siskin, Clifford. *Work of Writing: Literature and Social Change in Britain, 1700-1830*. Baltimore and London: Johns Hopkins UP, 1998.

Small, Christopher. *The Printed Word: An Instrument of Popularity*. Aberdeen: U of Aberdeen P, 1982.

Spufford, Margaret. *Small Books and Pleasant Histories: Popular Fiction and its Readership in Seventeenth Century England*. Athens, GA: U of Georgia P, 1982.

Sydney, Sir Philip. *The Psalms of Sir Philip Sidney and the Countess of Pembroke, ed. J.C.A Rathmell*. NY: Yale UP, 1963.

Ulrich, Laurel Thatcher. *Good Wives: Image and Reality in the Lives of Women in Northern New England 1650-1750*. New York: Vintage Books, 1991.

Watts, Emily Stipes. *The Poetry of American Women From 1632 to 1945*. Austin and London: U of Texas P, 1977.

Walker, Cheryl. "Anne Bradstreet: A Woman Poet." *Critical Essays on Anne Bradstreet*. Ed. Pattie Cowell and Ann Stanford.

Wall, Wendy. *The Imprint of Gender: Authorship and Publication in the English Renaissance*. Ithaca and London: Cornell UP, 1993.

Wheatley, Phillis. *Complete Writings*. Ed. and Intro. Vincent Carretta. NY: Penguin, 2001.

White, Elizabeth Wade. *Anne Bradstreet: "The Tenth Muse"*. NY: Oxford UP, 1971.

Wilcox, Kristin. "The Body into Print: Marketing Phillis Wheatley." *American Literature* 71, 1999.

Willard, Carla. "Wheatley's Turn of Praise: Heroic Entrapment and the Paradox of Revolution." *American Literature 67, 1995*.

Winthrop, John. *Winthrop Papers*. 5 vols. Boston: Massachusetts Historical Society, 1931.

Wiseman, Susan. *Drama, Politics, in the English Civil War*. Cambridge, UK; NY: Cambridge UP, 1998.

Wrightson, Keith. *English Society, 1580-1680*. New Brunswick, NJ: Rutgers UP, 1982.

Index

Breinigsville, PA USA
20 August 2010
243942BV00002B/1/P